Conversations in Excellence
Integrating Mission

edited by Joseph O'Keefe, S.J. and Regina Haney

A Component of SPICE: **S**elected **P**rograms for **I**mproving **C**atholic **E**ducation, a national diffusion network for Catholic schools.

371.071273
C76

Copyright 1997 National Catholic Educational Association
1077 30th Street, NW, Suite 100
Washington, DC 20007-3852
ISBN 1-55833-194-8

Contents

5 Preface

7 Chapter One
The Call to Collaboration
Joseph M. O'Keefe, S.J.

17 Chapter Two
SPICE: Overview and Plans for the Future
Regina Haney

27 Chapter Three
The Schools and Their Programs
Larry Bowman and Carol Cimino, S.S.J.

39 Chapter Four
Integrating Mission into the
Life of Institutions
Mary M Brabeck, Otherine Neisler, Nancy Zollers

57 Chapter Five
Mission and Catholic Education:
Theological Perspectives
Margaret Eletta Guider, O.S.F.

71 Chapter Six
Motivating for Change and Renewal
Robert R. Bimonte, F.S.C..

Preface

Conversations in Excellence: Integrating Mission is the first volume in a series of annual NCEA publications that will allow a wide audience to participate in SPICE (**S**elected **P**rograms for **I**mproving **C**atholic **E**ducation). SPICE is a process that identifies, validates, and systematically diffuses elementary and secondary school programs that work so that teachers and/or administrators in other schools can adapt them. Each year has its own theme. In 1996 the theme was "integrating mission into the life of the school;" in 1997, "how Catholic schools creatively provide for the diverse needs of children and their families;" and in 1998, "creative financing and resourcing of Catholic schools." Conversations in Excellence, a conference held at Boston College each summer, provides principals and teachers the opportunity to present their program, to receive feedback from colleagues, and to gain new perspectives from experts. By offering proceedings from the conference as well as other invited papers, the *Conversations in Excellence* series is designed to provide Catholic and non-Catholic educators with a resource for school renewal.

Conversations in Excellence would never have taken place without financial support from the Father Michael J. McGivney Memorial Fund for New Initiatives in Catholic Education, the Chief Administrators of Catholic Education (CACE) Research Center Board and two publishers: Silver Burdett Ginn and William H. Sadlier. Boston College provided personnel, facilities, and funding for Conversations in Excellence through the efforts of Rev. J. Donald Monan, S.J. (Chancellor), Rev. William Neenan, S.J. (Academic Vice President), Rev. Michael Buckley, S.J. (Director of the Jesuit Institute), and Rev. Joseph Appleyard, S.J. (Rector of the Jesuit Community).

Many people at NCEA have given time and support to this effort, especially Michael Guerra and Mary Frances Taymans, S.N.D. (Department of Secondary Schools), Robert Kealey and Antoinette Dudek, O.S.F. (Department of Elementary Schools), Dale McDonald, P.B.V.M. (Public Policy Research Associate), and Fran Freeman (Department of Chief Administrators of Catholic Education).

Boston College faculty have likewise volunteered time and effort, especially Mary Brabeck (Dean of the School of Education), Martha Bronson (Associate Professor, Department of Counseling, Developmental Psychology and Research Methods), Nancy Zollers and Otherine Neisler (Assistant Professors, Department of Curriculum, Administration and Special Education), and Mary Ellen Harmon, R.S.C.J (Senior Research Associate, Center for the Study of Testing, Evaluation and Educational Policy).

Catholic educators from across the country have generously provided leadership for SPICE. Among them are: Robert Bimonte, F.S.C. (Superintendent of Education, Diocese of Buffalo, NY), Lawrence M. Bowman (Director for Catholic Education, Diocese of Covington, Kentucky), Thomas Butler (Superintendent of Schools, Diocese of Sacramento, California), Carol Cimino, S.S.J. (Director, Catholic School Administrators' Association of New York), Nancy Erhart (Curriculum Enhancer, Cathedral-Carmel School in Lafayette, Louisiana), Judy Ford (Director of Instructional Services, Archdiocese of Seattle, Washington), James McCloskey, C.S.Sp. (President, Holy Ghost Preparatory School, Ben-Salem, Pennsylvania), Frank X. Savage (Direction of Education and Life-long Formation, Diocese of Birmingham, Alabama), Michael J. Skube (Superintendent of Schools, Diocese of Charlotte, North Carolina), Barbara Swanson (Associate Superintendent, Diocese of Jefferson City, Missouri) and Leann Welch, P.B.V.M. (Superintendent of Schools, Diocese of Birmingham, Alabama).

Chapter 1

The Call to Collaboration

–Joseph M. O'Keefe, S. J.

On August 14, 1995, the Associated Press put on the wires a story printed in the *Boston Globe* the previous day. The story reports the following:

Roman Catholic educators want to spread the gospel of what works in their schools, but first they have to find out what those things are...During the next four years, they want to identify about 30 promising programs in such things as using technology, involving parents, including children with disabilities, and integrating Catholic values. The goal is to list as many successful programs as possible and to print the list in Catholic publications and make it available through computers.

The story refers to a gathering the previous weekend that gave birth to SPICE (Selected Programs for Improving Catholic Education). In Chapter Two Regina Haney describes in some detail the beginning and subsequent history of the program. This chapter will focus on the central elements of the philosophy that underlies SPICE, as well as the challenges it faces. The chapter concludes with an overview of each subsequent chapter in the book, as well as biographical information about the authors.

The logic behind SPICE appeals to common sense: rebuilding the wheel is a waste of energy and time. A five-step process insures that practitioners can learn from practitioners in order to reform schools. SPICE is designed to:

1. Find programs that address important problems or needs;
2. Assess their effectiveness through eternal and impartial review;
3. Create precise and user-friendly descriptions;
4. Make these descriptions available to a wider public through conferences and publications, on paper or in cyberspace;
5. Train those who created and/or maintain the program to become staff development providers for others.

SPICE developers are not the first people to have these insights into effective school renewal. In 1974 the Federal Government began the National Diffusion Network [NDN]. By the last year of its full operation (1993-1994), NDN had identified over 200 programs that were adapted in more than 35,000 public and private (including Catholic) schools in all fifty states, the District of Columbia, Puerto Rico, Virgin Islands, Guam, American Samoa, Palau, and the Commonwealth of Northern Mariana Islands. Program organizers estimate that over 141,000 persons received inservice training to the ultimate benefit of an estimated 6.3 million students. In the 1993-1994 academic year, active programs were classified into fifteen domains: preservice/inservice training, organizational reform, dropout prevention/alternative programs, reading/writing, humanities, mathematics, science/technology, social sciences, health/physical sciences, multidisciplinary/cognitive skills, early childhood/parent involvement, special education, gifted/talented, education for special populations (adult, higher education, migrant education), and career/vocational education. The major source of dissemination was an annual publication entitled *Programs That Work* (Lang, 1995).

The National Diffusion Network was one of the casualties of the recent massive budget cuts in federal domestic spending. At the August 1995 gathering, NDN leaders encouraged SPICE developers to carry on this important work. They were confident that two fundamental elements that distinguish SPICE from NDN will insure success: its university affiliation and its Catholic identity.

From its inception, SPICE has been co-sponsored by Boston College. Like all collaborative efforts, those between schools and universities are challenging. Each entity has its own goals, ways of proceeding, and fiscal constraints. Current developments within academia, however, provide a new impetus for collaboration. The heart of a university is scholarly inquiry. Until the recent past, scholars made sharp distinctions between pure and applied knowledge. The creation of "pure knowledge" was the work of the university; the insights and experience of people in the field counted for little. Not so today. Narrow and rigid definitions of the central work of the university are giving way to new forms of inquiry that blend theory and practice. Many describe this phenomenon as "action research." Richard Lerner (1995) calls it "outreach scholarship." The late Ernest L. Boyer was perhaps the most famous advocate of this new approach. He enumerated four equally worthwhile elements of scholarship: discovery, integration, teaching, and application. Of the latter he wrote, "Such a view of scholarly service — one that both applies and contributes to human knowledge — is particularly needed in a world in which huge, almost intractable problems call for the skills and insights only the academy can provide." He then quoted Oscar Handlin's belief that the world "can no longer afford the luxury of pursuits confined to an ivory tower....[S]cholarship has to prove its worth not on its own terms but by service to the nation and the world." (Boyer, 1990, p. 23)

The three organizational entities that make up SPICE — the National Catholic Educational Association, Boston College, and individual schools — vary greatly. However, no matter how great the differences of size, scope and structure, they share one mission that grows out of their Catholic identity. The schools involved, the national agency that is bringing them together, and the university that is partnered in the effort all share a particular understanding of how society should organize itself. Two major elements of Catholic social teaching — subsidiarity and solidarity — form the philosophical rationale for the system we have created.

The principle of subsidiarity teaches that the preferable arena of decision-making and action is local. Human dignity is served better by families, neighborhoods, and local communities than by large, impersonal, bureaucratic structures. The church has recently reaffirmed the conviction that one must oppose all forms of collectivism (Catechism, 1994, #1886, #1988) and that larger entities must exercise restraint (Catechism, 1994, #2209). The principal of subsidiarity was first articulated by Pope Pius XII in response to totalitarianism, but its application is much broader. It is often said that the term "Catholic school system" is a misnomer; it is, in fact, a "system of schools." The benefits of relative autonomy are many including: flexibility to respond to local exigencies, ability to try innovative programs, and a sense of community and empowerment of local administrators and teachers. In the most important recent study of Catholic schools, Bryk and his associates identify the importance of subsidiarity. The role of centralized organizations is not one of dominance but service: "Rather than regulating human activity under the homogenizing norms of a central bureaucracy, the role of external governance is to facilitate and stimulate collective local action." (Bryk, 1996, pp. 30-31)

Subsidiarity is a central tenet of the SPICE philosophy. The program is completely voluntary and model programs are not to be mass-produced or superimposed rigidly on the local scene. Each school must learn from another, assess local circumstances, and apply the knowledge where appropriate. While subsidiarity is key, too much of a good thing is no longer a good thing. Stress on the importance of the local, the small-scale, and the particular must be complemented by a kind of solidarity that is more universal in scope. This wider solidarity is essential, "...the quest for community is to avoid becoming a source of increased conflict in a world already riven by narrowness of vision." (Hollenbach, 1996, p. 94)

The relative autonomy of the Catholic school has its down side: time and energy are wasted reinventing the wheel, administrators and teachers get mired in everyday survival, and the universal nature of the Church becomes obscured. Solidarity is not simply a pragmatic response to social crisis; it is an imperative that flows from the Catholic understanding of the nature of God:

> "Beyond human and natural bonds, already so close and strong, there is discerned in the light of faith a new model of the unity of the human race, which must ultimately inspire solidarity. This supreme model of unity, which is a reflection of the intimate life of God, one God in three Persons, is what we Christians mean by the word communion." (John Paul II, 1987, #40, p. 75)

The Catholic "big C" notion of solidarity is catholic "small c" in its embrace of all people, regardless of where they are. If I am a teacher in a Catholic school in New Mexico, I am in some sense responsible for students in Maine. The principal of a Catholic school in Los Angeles must care about the struggles of teachers in New York. SPICE relies on the deep-seated conviction of Catholic educators that precious time and energy belongs not only to "my" kids, but to everybody's kids. We believe that Tom Groome is correct when he asserts that "Catholic education is often countercultural to the mores of rugged individualism, self-sufficiency, and social indifference that permeate Western society." (Groome, 1996, p. 116)

The forces that can diminish Catholic identity generally can also destroy SPICE. Two are particularly relevant: unrestrained self-interest and short-term thinking. The uncontrolled market model of education reform, which sadly is embraced by many Catholic educators, is particularly problematic. Competition is the order of the day: be number one at all costs, get higher in the rankings, find a monopolistic niche, and measure all initiatives by the question, "What's in it for me?" It is indeed tragic to see Catholic schools and universities give in to the temptation to compete with each other for students, scarce resources, and publicity. Gerald Grace (1996, p. 70) describes the situation:

> Catholic schools in many societies are working in social, political and ideological conditions which challenge fundamentally their distinctive educational mission and their historical educational commitments. In these present contexts,

> a Catholic conception of education as primarily moral and spiritual, concerned with principled behavior and focused upon community and public good outcomes faces a major challenge from New Right conceptions of education which are aggressively market oriented and individualistic in approach. (Grace, 1996, p. 70)

When Catholic educators become forgetful of a faith perspective, profit margin replaces mission and the goal is to be a winner at any price. In this scenario, practitioners will be unwilling to spend time and effort to help others learn about their success; in fact, they may want to keep the good news to themselves exclusively lest they lose superiority over sister institutions. Without principals and teachers taking the effort to send in applications, the program is doomed. Likewise, NCEA officials and university faculty may be unwilling to give of themselves in the long term. SPICE requires a great deal of intensive work (usually pro bono) from many busy people. It takes time, energy, and money to publicize SPICE, assess programs, run conferences, and write an edited book each year, not to mention raising funds for program initiatives. SPICE relies on the fundamental solidarity of all Catholic educators.

An example of the short-term thinking that can diminish SPICE is what many call "the tyranny of the immediate." Engaging in school reform is like trying to redesign a 747 while it is in flight. This is especially true for principals, who are central players in the SPICE initiative. Roland Barth (1990, pp. 72-73) describes the situation:

> Like most who work in schools these days, principals walk a narrow edge between being able and not being able to fulfill their complex job. Exhaustion and discouragement are high; discretionary time and energy are low. In such a climate, opportunities to participate in a new activity, even one addressed to the principal's own renewal, entail risks and demand that the principal give up something to make room for the new activity or else risk becoming further overextended and depleted. A major paradox confronting any who would assist principals as well as teachers in becoming learners in their schools, then, is that professional development is energy and time depleting as well as energy and time replenishing.

Despite the best of intentions, practitioners often find themselves saying, "Let me just get through the day."

I have recently completed a comprehensive survey of urban Catholic schools, with the ultimate aim of forming alliances and networks that will insure the survival of this vital ministry in the church. A number of principals wrote to me indicating that they simply cannot take the time to engage in a project whose outcome is uncertain or long-term. An East Coast principal wrote, "...the typical inner-city principal is on a constant crisis schedule in addition to the everyday care of a school." One from the Midwest described a near impossible task: "I am the bookkeeper, secretary, banker, accountant, budget person, etc. I am in the process of going through a school budget for the diocese. The school has a significant deficit. We have a free lunch program, as well as before- and after-school day care. I have to take care of it all." Another from the Midwest wrote, "This survey was extremely time-consuming. Please do not ask us to participate in any follow-up. We must be about our daily ministry." From the West Coast I read: "In the inner city Catholic school we do not have a great deal of personnel to go around. It is extremely difficult for a principal to take time out from a super busy schedule to answer a survey or fill out additional forms."

Despite the difficulties of a radically individualistic culture and the daunting tasks of teaching and administration, the Church calls her educators to see beyond the here and now. In the decree on education from the Second Vatican Council (1966, p. 737, #12) one reads:

> As cooperation, which is becoming daily more important and more effective at diocesan, national, and international levels, is very necessary also in the educational sphere, every care should be taken to encourage suitable coordination between Catholic schools. Such collaboration between these and other schools, as the welfare of the whole community requires, should also be developed.

Ten years later, the Church reiterated the call for collaboration: "Today especially one sees a world which clamors for solidarity and yet experiences the rise of new forms of individualism. Society can take note from the Catholic school that it is possible to create true communities out of a common effort for the common good." (Sacred Congregation for Christian Education, 1977, p. 620, # 62) Catholic universities, like the schools, must respond to the call for collaboration. The Holy Father wrote in *Ex corde ecclesiae* (1992):

> Through programs of continuing education offered to the wider community, by making its scholars available for consulting services, by taking advantage of modern means of communication, and in a variety of other ways, a Catholic university can assist in making the growing body of human knowledge and a developing understanding of the faith available to a wider public, thus expanding university services beyond its own academic community.

The call to collaboration comes not only from the *Magisterium*. A principal from the Midwest bemoaned the length of my recent survey, but then added, "I think it's worth the effort. Catholic schools need to begin thinking of themselves as a whole — not a bunch of schools." Likewise, a principal from the East wrote:

> I would like to see a convention with all the Catholic elementary schools in the U.S. from the inner city (especially those schools with high percentages of African-American students and other minority groups). Our schools are a beacon of hope to many communities, yet our struggle for survival is greater each year. We could gain so much from each other. Sharing our resources and networks would be of benefit to all schools involved. The convention would also give us strength and support of knowing that we are all in the struggle of survival together for our children.

Conclusion

SPICE hopes to spread the gospel of what works in schools, but cannot do so without remembering the Gospel that is their source and inspiration. Building on the experience of the National Diffusion Network, informed by expanded notions of scholarly inquiry, rooted in the principles of subsidiarity and solidarity, Catholic educators can indeed overcome the forces of self-interest and short-term thinking that destroy educational rejuvenation. With God's grace and hard work, SPICE can provide Catholic educators at all levels and in all locations "...the strength and support of knowing that we are all in a struggle of survival together for our children."

Overview of the Book

This volume provides the reader with an introduction to SPICE through publication of the proceedings of the first annual Conversations in Excellence. In Chapter Two, Regina Haney, Co-Director of SPICE and Director of NABE, the National Association of Boards of Education of the NCEA, provides a history of SPICE and an overview of its process and plans for the future. In Chapter Three, Sister Carol Cimino, CSJ, Director of the Catholic School Administrative Association of New York, and Larry Bowman, Superintendent of Schools in the Covington Kentucky Diocese, present the seven 1996 SPICE schools and their programs. They describe the program focus, goals, activities and plans for implementation. Chapter Four is co-authored by three Boston College faculty members: Mary Brabeck, Dean of the School of Education and Professor of Counseling and Developmental Psychology, Otherine Neisler, Assistant Professor in Teacher Education and Nancy Zollers, also Assistant Professor in Teacher Education. They too discuss the call to collaboration by recounting Boston College's experience in on-campus interprofessional development as well as partnerships with local schools. Sr. Margaret Eletta Guider, OSF, Professor of Religion and Society at Weston Jesuit School of Theology, wrote Chapter Five, "Mission and Catholic Education: Theological Perspectives." She describes the church's teaching about the unequaled importance of children. In Chapter Six, Brother Robert Bimonte, FSC, Superintendent of Education for the Diocese of Buffalo, explores the nature of rigidity and then offers four requirements for successful change.

References

Barth, R. S. (1990). *Improving Schools from Within*. San Francisco: Jossey-Bass.

Boyer, E. L. (1990). *Scholarship Reconsidered: Priorities of the Professoriate*. Princeton, NJ: The Carnegie Foundation for the Advancement of Teaching.

Bryk, A.S. (1996). Lessons from Catholic High Schools for Renewing Our Educational Institutions. In McLaughlin, T.H., O'Keefe, J. M. & O'Keeffe, B., (Eds.) *The Contemporary Catholic School: Context, Identity and Diversity*. London, Washington: Falmer. 25-41.

Catechism of the Catholic Church (1994). London: Geoffrey Chapman.

Grace, G. (1996). Leadership in Catholic Schools. In McLaughlin, T.H., O'Keefe, J. M. & O'Keeffe, B., (Eds.) *The Contemporary Catholic School: Context, Identity and Diversity*. London, Washington: Falmer. 70-88.

Groome, T. H. (1996). What Makes a School Catholic? In McLaughlin, T.H., O'Keefe, J. M. & O'Keeffe, B., (Eds.) *The Contemporary Catholic School: Context, Identity and Diversity*. London, Washington: Falmer. 107-125.

Hollenbach, D. (1996). The Common Good, Pluralism and the Catholic School. In McLaughlin, T.H., O'Keefe, J. M. & O'Keeffe, B., (Eds.) *The Contemporary Catholic School: Context, Identity and Diversity*. London, Washington: Falmer. 289-103.

Lang, G. (Ed.) (1995). *Education Programs that Work: The Catalogue of the National Diffusion Network*. Longmont, CO: Sopris West.

Lerner, R. M. (1995). *America's Youth in Crisis: Challenges and Options for Programs and Policies*. Thousand Oaks, CA: SAGE Publications.

Pope John Paul II. (1987). *On Social Concern (Solicitudo rei socialis)*. Boston: St. Paul Books.

Pope John Paul II. (1992). Ex Corde Ecclesiae. In Gallin, A. (Ed.). *American Catholic Higher Education: Essential Documents*, 1967-1990. Notre Dame, IN: University of Notre Dame Press. 413-437.

Sacred Congregation for Christian Education. (1977). *Malgré les déclarations*. In Flannery, A. (Ed.). *Vatican Council II: More Post-Conciliar Documents*. Volume II. Northport, NY: Costello Publishing.

Vatican Council II. (1965). Declaration on Christian Education. In Flannery, A. (Ed.). *Vatican Council II: More Post-Conciliar Documents*. Volume II. Northport, NY: Costello Publishing.

Chapter 2

SPICE: Overview and Plans for the Future

–Regina Haney

The proceedings from the first Conversations in Excellence, conducted in July 1996, are captured in this publication. Seven teams of three from Catholic schools were selected to converse with one another, Boston College professors, staff development consultants, Catholic education diocesan and local administrators, and Dr. Robert Coles, noted child psychiatrist, author, and professor at Harvard University. The topic of the conversations was integration of the mission into all aspects of the school life, including extracurricular activities and athletic programs.

The purpose of this book is to capture those conversations so that educators might glean insights from the wisdom of others to better provide quality Catholic education for those whom they serve. More specifically, through this volume, the National Catholic Educational Association (NCEA) and Boston College continue to encourage participation in Selected Programs for Improving Catholic Education (SPICE). This is a process that assists Catholic educators to identify, validate, and systematically diffuse Catholic elementary and secondary school programs that work so that teachers and/or administrators in other schools can adapt them.

The six chapters of this book are written by the SPICE planning committee (those who developed SPICE) and presenters at the first Conversations in Excellence. Three of the chapters are modifications of formal presentations delivered during the four-day conference that focused on the integration of the school's mission.

Genesis of SPICE

For the National Catholic Educational Association, the largest Catholic education membership organization, the mission "to provide leadership and service to all those in Catholic education" drives the organization to identify and carry out programs and activities that will provide the best for those served. Its members serve in preschools and kindergartens, in elementary and secondary schools, in colleges and universities, in religious education programs and in seminaries. Although the students in these classes are diverse in age and background, the overall mission–to deliver the word of God–is singular.

A membership organization founded in 1904, the National Catholic Educational Association, represents 200,000 educators serving 7.6 million students in Catholic elementary and secondary schools, religious education programs, seminaries, and universities. Because Selected Programs for Improving Catholic Education (SPICE) provides direction and assistance to Catholic elementary and secondary educators looking to adapt programs that work, it taps into one of the Catholic school's strengths—helping one another by sharing. Catholic educators have often heard about interesting new Catholic school programs through word of mouth, but have had no way to systematically evaluate and learn from them.

In the past, our Catholic schools accessed exemplar educational programs from the National Diffusion Network. For over 20 years the National Diffusion Network was the only national educational, dissemination system in the country. It offered schools of the United States proven public school programs that demonstrated their effectiveness in improving student performance, lent themselves to use in a variety of educational settings, and were reasonable in cost. Catholic schools use the NDN resources offered by the United States Department of Education; for example, the Archdiocese of Philadelphia, adapted an NDN-approved program, Staff Development Designed for Designers of Learning. NDN assisted and supported over 1,200 Catholic educators throughout five counties in the archdiocese to be a "designer of learning rather than a conveyor of information" as they learned to design curricula that they would be using. Because of a severe cut in funds, NDN's efforts are presently limited.

SPICE differs from the NDN in that it is a national Catholic education dissemination system and the proven programs are Catholic school programs, not public school programs. It is directed by the National Catholic Educational Association and Boston College, not the U.S. Department of Education, and appropriately so, because the purpose of SPICE is to assist Catholic educators to provide quality Catholic education.

For Catholic education at this time, sharing resources is more important than ever. New Catholic school models are needed to meet the needs of changing families, church, and society. Private funding resources are dwindling while education costs continue to rise. Catholic education has many successful models across the United States. Some of them have been identified by the U.S. Department of Education through the Blue Ribbon School Awards program, while others are yet to be discovered. SPICE intends to gather these successful programs and, through a diffusion network, make them available to schools in need of successful programs.

The idea for a Catholic diffusion network came out of the National Congress on Catholic Schools for the 21st Century. The two-year process (1989-1991) involved Catholic educators nationwide. During this time, 19 regional meetings were held at which participants surfaced future major issues facing them in the areas of Catholic Identity; Catholic Schools and Society; Catholic School Governance and Finance; Leadership in and on Behalf of Catholic Schools; Political Action, and Public Policy and Catholic Schools. The process concluded with a gathering of 250 delegates in Washington, DC. Many of the delegates had participated in the regional meetings and included representatives from all groups in the Catholic school community: bishops, clergy, vicars of education, superintendents of schools, principals, teachers, school boards, home school associations, colleges and universities, researchers, business, and public service. As a result of their five-day effort, delegates provided belief and direction statements to ensure the future of Catholic education.

One of the five directional statements for Catholic Schools and Society makes it clear that it will take "new models to meet the needs of changing families, church, and society." As we shape Catholic schools for the 21st Century, we also want to respond to the call of the Congress to identify and share these new models and ideas as expressed in the Epilogue, "to use the wisdom and talent we have to build a stronger and larger network of Catholic schools; now is the time to invite others to share today's tasks and tomorrow's dreams."

The Congress' challenge was taken up by the Supervision, Personnel and Curriculum (SPC) advisory committee of the Chief Administrators of Catholic Education (CACE), a department of NCEA. The advisory committee is representative of the SPC membership who, for the most part, are assistant-superintendents or superintendents in diocesan offices dealing with elementary and secondary teacher supervision, curriculum and personnel issues. For two years the committee sought program development funding. During the academic year 1993-94, the committee found two inestimable resources, the CACE Research Center Board and Boston College. The board awarded funds as well as support by offering to market the program in their home regions. Boston College offered to cosponsor the project with NCEA by committing financial and human resources.

Over a weekend in August 1995, three members of the SPC advisory committee–Tom Butler, assistant superintendent, Diocese of Madison, WI; Carol Cimino,SSJ, assistant director,

Catholic School Administrators' Association, Troy, NY; and Barbara Swanson, associate superintendent, Diocese of Jefferson City, MO–convened a group of Catholic educators to design a program that would systematically identify new models of effective Catholic elementary and secondary programs for Catholic educators to adapt. Delegates from CACE and the elementary and secondary departments of NCEA joined Boston College faculty members and other leaders in Catholic education to act on the challenge and invitation of the National Congress. They created SPICE. The three members of the SPC advisory committee who convened the planning group were joined by representatives from the NCEA school-related departments as well as Boston College faculty members. Their names and positions are presented in the preface.

At the August meeting, this planning committee studied and discussed the pros and cons of the National Diffusion Network with the assistance of Frank Delany, director, and Fay O'Brien, assistant director of The Private School Facilitator Project of The National Diffusion Network. Taking the best from this system of access to validated public school programs, the committee crafted a Catholic school diffusion network.

The committee identified ten focus areas that are essential if they are to have quality Catholic schools in the twenty-first century. These are: integration of the mission; technology; parent/guardian involvement; inclusion of students with diverse needs; middle schools within a K-8 setting; a K-12 religious instruction; governance structures; financial development; instructional leaders; non-college bound students. The committee next explored possible ways to organize Catholic educators to communicate and share with other Catholic practitioners. Program components were developed along with the application process. Lastly, the group designed a plan to finance and publicize the program.

Conversations in Excellence 1996

In the spring of 1996, the planning committee's dream became a reality. Selected Catholic elementary and secondary schools with exemplar programs that integrate the mission in all facets of school life were invited to apply for participation in the first SPICE activity, 1996 Conversations in Excellence. In inaugurating this initial selection process, the committee decided to recruit schools recognized by the U.S. Department of Education Blue Ribbon School Program, since integration of mission is one of the program's criteria for selection. Catholic educators who served as Blue Ribbon site visitors were contacted and asked to nominate award-winning Catholic schools that they had visited. With the support of area superintendents of schools, these schools were invited to apply. Of those that accepted the invitation, seven were chosen by a review panel. The seven schools were: St. Rocco School, Johnston, RI; Holy Names Academy, Seattle, WA; St. Mark, St. Jude, and St. Lawrence Schools, Indianapolis, IN; Ursuline Academy, New York, NY; and Matignon High School, Cambridge, MA.

Teams of three from each of these schools gathered at Boston College in July 1996 for the first Conversations in Excellence. They shared their "Integration of the Mission" success stories with other practitioners, academicians, researchers and other professionals from the educational community.

"Success is a process, not a destination." The seven SPICE school teams were reminded of this by the Conversations in Excellence presenters and process. Each presenter made significant suggestions that raised the bar for excellence and effectiveness for each of the seven schools. Robert Coles spoke on "The Mission of Education," reminding the participants that the staff must be models of the mission. Mary Brabeck, Ph.D., Dean of the School of Education at Boston College, spoke on "Integrating Mission into the Life of Institutions: Psychological Perspectives." Dr. Brabeck challenged participants to go beyond the school community to build partnerships with other institutions, agencies, and services. Such partners would provide invaluable assistance in the school's efforts to integrate the mission across the life of the school. Margaret Guider, OSF, spoke on "Integrating Mission into the Life of Institutions: Theological Perspectives." Sister Guider talked about what the church really believes about the importance of children. One of the criteria for recognition as a SPICE school is the commitment to provide training for the adapting schools. Denise Blumenthal, a consultant known for her work with the National Diffusion Network, and Brother Robert Bimonte, FSC, gave sessions that focused on assisting SPICE teams to prepare training modules.

Throughout the three days, the teams were provided with opportunities to showcase their programs. On Friday afternoon, a Poster Session was presented during which Catholic educators from the surrounding area interacted with the teams to hear first-hand about their programs. The teams spent most of Saturday revising their programs in light of the presentations and feedback, as well as preparing staff-development plans for the adapting schools. On Sunday, each team presented an overview of their staff development plans.

The first Conversations in Excellence program concluded with liturgy celebrated with J.Donald Monan, SJ, Chancellor of Boston College. Father Monan presented each team with a certificate recognizing their school as a SPICE school, one with an exemplary program that can be adapted by other Catholic schools nationwide.

Hopes for the Future

The 1996 Conversations in Excellence successfully tested and launched several of the components of SPICE. Exemplary and validated programs do exist in our Catholic schools. School personnel are amenable to showcasing such programs as seen by their willingness to apply and participate. They also are willing and poised to assist others to adapt the programs. Funders, those holding the purse strings, support planning for and testing of new initiatives. In this instance, both the CACE Research Center Board and Boston College supported the August 1995 planning session. Boston College and Catholic education publishers invested in the experimental or initial Conversations in Excellence.

The program has a very simple application process. Will schools voluntarily apply for participation or will they have to be solicited to apply as were those for the 1996 program? It seems that a combination of both is needed until the program is established. One suggestion for addressing this problem is to involve the SPC advisory committee which is made up of regional representatives. Each of the 12 representatives can be responsible for encouraging and assisting at least one school in the region to apply.

The database of exemplar programs is presently limited to the seven schools that participated last summer. These programs are posted on the NCEA web-site and have been disseminated to all Catholic schools and diocesan offices through a flyer. Hopefully, this publicity will not only increase the number of schools adapting the programs, but will also encourage schools to apply and participate in the SPICE program.

At the 1997 Annual NCEA Convention in Minneapolis, the 1996 SPICE schools were invited to present their programs and this will continue as a motivator for other schools to participate in SPICE. In addition to getting schools to apply, program organizers face many challenges as they implement the three final components of the program: 1. Train trainers to help schools to replicate SPICE programs; 2. Create self-instruction packages, including videos; 3. Secure finances for ongoing activities.

Administrators and teachers already have more than a full plate of responsibilities. SPICE school personnel have, therefore, little or no time to develop training programs. The challenge to the program directors will be to build adequate time into the Conversations in Excellence program to draft a training program. Beginning with the 1997 SPICE schools, directors and consultants (funded through SPICE) will work with the school teams throughout the year to finalize the training programs. The directors will develop self-instructional packages from these programs.

Financing ongoing activities is another challenge. As was mentioned earlier, start-up money is easier to attract. Revenue from training sessions, and publication sales from books such as this are part of the SPICE business plan. Such revenue will not, however, totally support the needed staff at the national level as the program grows, nor will this level of income provide incentives for schools to apply or to support schools that need travel scholarships in order to attend the program at Boston College. To get foundations and individual donors to finance the operations is difficult. This is a challenge for the directors.

Project administrators expect to identify 30 promising school programs over the next year in such areas as meeting the needs of children and their families, technology use, parent involvement, inclusion of children with learning disabilities, and integration of Catholic values. A database of validated programs along with training in-service and materials to adapt programs that integrate the school's mission and meet the needs of children and their families will be created.

The call from the National Congress makes it clear that it will take new models to meet the needs of changing families, church, and society. The SPICE program is a response to the call to network schools to identify and adapt exemplary Catholic school programs.

Chapter 3

The Schools and Their Programs

—Larry Bowman and Carol Cimino, S.S.J.

The central activity of Conversations in Excellence was the sharing of the schools' outstanding programs. Seven schools from around the country were invited to showcase their programs and to devise ways in which their program could be adopted and adapted by other Catholic schools. The schools invited to do this were: St. Rocco School, Johnston, RI; Holy Names Academy, Seattle, WA; St. Mark School, Indianapolis, IN; St. Jude School, Indianapolis, IN; St. Lawrence School, Indianapolis, IN; The Ursuline School, New Rochelle, NY; and Matignon Catholic High School, Cambridge, MA.

This chapter will be devoted to a brief summary of each of the school's program focus, program goals, program activities and program implementation, or suggested steps to replicate the program in other schools. Keep in mind that, since the overall focus of the 1996 Conversations in Excellence was Integration of the Mission, each of the following programs seeks to point out that focus area in explaining the steps it took toward developing the program. The following is a summary of each of the school's offerings.

St. Rocco School, Johnston, RI

St. Rocco School is an elementary school located in a middle-class suburb of Providence. The mission of the school is closely identified with the religious order that staffs the school, the Apostles of the Sacred Heart of Jesus. The program highlighted is integral to the mission of the school: "Sharing the Love of the Heart of Christ".

Program Focus: Integration of the mission statement into all aspects of school life, including extracurricular activities and athletic programs. The program provides examples of various ways in which the mission statement is lived out through in-service projects involving students and volunteer parents and the integration of service activities and their values into the curriculum.

Program Goals: According to the staff of the school, the goals of the program are to: "identify, live, integrate the mission of St. Rocco School." The school, after identifying its mission, discussed strategies for communicating it and integrating it into the total life of the school. The phrase from the mission statement, "Sharing the Love of the Heart of Christ" is literally used everywhere in the school and on all its publications. It has become a marketing strategy as well and all parts of the school community have daily reminders of the mission of the school.

Program Activities:
a. The mission statement is read at the beginning of each faculty meeting, Home-School Association meeting, student assembly, and school board meeting.

b. Students are expected to commit the mission statement to memory.
   c. The school, including the classrooms, is decorated with signs, symbols and words of the mission statement, and photos on display show tangible signs of the integration of school activities with the mission. In addition, all printed materials connected with the school have the mission "Sharing the Love of the Heart of Christ" included.

Implementing the Program: It is essential that the faculty and staff explore the need to identify a mission. Brainstorming, focus groups, and other activities can help all components of the school community to decide what the school is all about. Next, the school must match, against the mission, all of its activities, curricular, co-curricular, and extracurricular. Members of the school need to ask:

   a. What does this program/activity have to do with our mission?
   b. How do we communicate the integration of the mission into all activities? What signs and symbols will we use ?
   c. How can we make sure that all future programs fit into the stated mission of the school?
   d. How can we ritualize, that is, develop liturgical and paraliturgical services that contextualize the mission?
   e. How do we communicate the mission to new members of the school community?

Holy Names Academy, Seattle, WA

Holy Names Academy is an all-girl secondary school conducted by the Sisters of the Holy Names of Jesus and Mary. The program highlighted deals with the integration of new teachers into the mission and the life of the school.

Program Focus: The new teacher mentoring program focuses on orientation to the school culture through an understanding of the mission and charism of the religious order and the unique educational mission of the school. The program has three components: pre-service before school begins, frequent instructional leadership in-service during the school year, and a mentor-teacher assignment.

Program Goals: The program is designed for teachers new to the school, both beginning teachers and teachers experienced in a different school environment. The goals are to help beginning teachers progress more rapidly and smoothly toward mastery of teaching, to educate all teachers new to the school in an understanding of the institutional culture, to prepare for the future by instructing new faculty/staff in the unique charism of the Sisters of the Holy Names of Jesus and Mary, in the Catholic identity, and in the specific educational mission of the school and to establish a strong relationship between new faculty and the instructional leadership team.

Program Activities:
   a. New teachers have a three-day inservice meeting prior to the regular pre-school inservice, including a day with the educational leaders at the Archdiocese so as to learn the context for a spiritual foundation for the school. The two days at the school consist of touring the building, meeting key faculty, staff and student leaders, examining the curriculum, role-playing the first day of school, and exploring the culture of the school.
   b. Weekly inservice of new teachers with instructional leaders allows new faculty members to debrief, ask questions, share observations, and explore issues on a regular basis.
   c. A team of master teachers is identified to make relatively frequent classroom observations, and provide direct, nonevaluative feedback and assistance to the new teachers.

Implementing the Program: Before implementing a new teacher mentoring program, the following must occur:

   a. Develop, adopt, and promulgate a clear and concise institutional mission statement.
   b. Identify the administrator who will direct the program. It is preferable that the administrator chosen is a master teacher with several years of experience in the school.
   c. Develop goals for the program.
   d. Convince all concerned parties of the need to invest resources in the teacher mentoring program.
   e. Invite several master teachers to assist with workshops and to act as mentors.

f. Involve current mentor teachers in the training of the next "generation of mentors".

g. Clarify program participation expectations with all new teachers at the time of hiring.

St. Mark School, Indianapolis, IN

St. Mark School is a K-8 elementary school within the Archdiocese of Indianapolis serving 350 students. The middle school program of the school is designed to meet the expectations of the school's mission statement, and is meant to be worked out in the K-8 setting.

Program Focus: A middle school concept is designed to meet the expectations of the mission statement in unique ways. Pre-adolescents and adolescents need to practice Catholic values, achieve academic success, and learn social responsibility. In addition to preparing students for the challenging curriculum of high school, the program provides a practical arts/exploratory arts curriculum focused to meet the academic, social, and physical challenges and changes the students are undergoing.

Program goals at St Mark School are to recognize the uniqueness of pre-adolescents and adolescents, to show these students that the school values who they are and how they are in a variety of ways, and to utilize what the school community knows about this age group to engage them in productive activities consistent with the mission of the school.

Program Activities:

a. Scheduling for grades 5 to 8 is done in blocks of 40 minutes for 9 blocks per day.

b. Students in grades 7 and 8 participate in the exploratory and practical arts program four days a week. The exploratory activities are French, German, Spanish, and Logic. The practical are Careers, Crafts, Woodworking, and Computer.

c. Student government is strengthened and provides service programs, principally, and social programs, secondarily.

d. Liturgies, prayer services, and other assemblies offer the opportunity for students in the middle grades to "buddy up"with students in the primary grades.

e. There is a Leadership Forum which consists of regular meetings of 7th and 8th graders to discuss school issues, solve problems, and develop service activities.

Program Implementation: It is necessary for all components of the school community to be in agreement on the implementation of this program, since it requires changes in scheduling, and different utilization of teacher time and skills.

  a. Discuss how implementing this program relates to the mission of the school.

  b. Determine what grades will be included.

  c. The exploratory arts and the practical arts program offerings will be determined by the resources, interests, and talents of staff, faculty, and volunteers.

  d. It is necessary to evaluate the program regularly so that the program's activities can be matched with the current needs of students.

St. Jude School, Indianapolis, IN

St. Jude School is a K-8 elementary school with an enrollment of 500 students. The school is a part of the Archdiocese of Indianapolis.

Program Focus: A diverse mix of "Enrichment Programs" collectively encompasses the goals of the mission statement of the school and enhance the curriculum.

Program Goals: In light of "To Teach As Jesus Did", the school states: In conjunction with the family and community, staff and faculty accept the responsibility:

  a. to provide each child with a challenging academic program rooted in the beliefs, values, and traditions of Catholic Christianity;

  b. to enable each child to discover and develop his/her God-given ability in mind, body, and spirit, so he/she may become a productive member of society;

  c. to guide each child in acquiring the skills, virtues, and habits of heart and mind that are required for effective service to God, self, and humankind;

d. to stimulate each child to reason and think, to be responsible for one's actions, and to make decisions based on Catholic/Christian values;

e. to keep pace with developments in educational technology and theory, in order to assess realistically changing student needs.

Program Activities: The enrichment program consists of the following activities in which the students of St. Jude School participate: Academic Olympics, Poetry Anthology, Ecology Camp, Careers Program, Choir/Show Choir, Eighth Grade Class trip, International Day, Jason Project (Marine Ecology), New Family Mentor Program, Midwest Talent Search, Service Projects, Quest for Excellence (student achievement), Student Newspaper, Forensic League, Spell Bowl, and Think Big (academic competition).

Implementing the Program: The activities selected need the following prerequisites to succeed: a. availability of faculty, staff, parents to supervise and/or implement the program; b. resources available in the local academic, civic, cultural community which can be utilized by the school at no or low cost; c. willingness on the part of the school community to integrate an enrichment program into the overall mission of the school.

St. Lawrence School, Indianapolis, IN

St. Lawrence School is an elementary, K-8 school with an enrollment of 400 students in the Archdiocese of Indianapolis.

Program Goals: The program highlights three interlocking dimensions of message, community, and service found in "To Teach As Jesus Did" and demonstrates how the St. Lawrence technology progam embraces those dimensions. The program also demonstrates how living-out these characteristics of a Catholic school enhance the Catholic identity of the school.

Program Activities:
a. Primary focus is given to the inservice of teachers so they become more technologically astute in the learning environment. All teachers are expected to learn and to teach with technology so inservice is provided to each staff member at every level. This inservice provides staff with

knowledge and skills to teach computers, use the laser disc, and materials in the math manipulatives library.

b. Primary teachers receive inservice in the Writing to Read Program which is the focus of the writing curriculum at that level.

c. The entire faculty is trained on the curriculum-based software which is on the school's network so they can utilize it to supplement the curriculum.

d. The staff uses the Excelsior Plus Grade Book. Those who have knowledge of it and feel comfortable with the program provide in-service to other staff members.

Implementing the Program:
a. Any program requires careful planning, and this is especially important to a technology program. The first suggestion to any school wishing to have a technology program is to assemble a group to do planning of resources and expenditures.

b. It is essential that the program have high interest in the community including that of students, teachers, administrators, parents, and extended community.

c. Financial support must be found. Grants, gifts, and donations may be used toward implementation of the program.

d. The efficacy of the program must always be measured against the mission of the school, and this measure must be used to evaluate the program.

The Ursuline School, New Rochelle, NY

Ursuline is a secondary girls' school conducted by the Ursuline Sisters which enrolls 650 students.

Program Focus: The focus is a peer counseling/peer mediation program for high school students. It seeks to further the mission of the school by involving students in a program which addresses issues of societal concerns to adolescents and devises ways to help them meet their own needs and those of their peers. In keeping with the philosophy of the school, it aims to develop in students the wisdom and discipline to make responsible choices.

Program Goals:
   a. To help students empower other students and, in particular, to empower women to be leaders in the community;
   b. To educate students to be citizens in the community and to learn the skills to make their lives successful: socially, academically, and personally. Specifically, in freshmen year, the program assists students to adjust to the high school environment. Students in the second year are trained as peer counselors and peer mediators.
   c. To help students to understand their own behavior and to be able to listen to and understand the needs of their peers;
   d. To learn that conflict is a normal part of living that can be used as an opportunity for learning and personal growth.
   e. To understand that since conflict is unavoidable, learning conflict resolution skills is as "educational and essential to the long-term success as learning science or a foreign language;"
   f. To encourage students to respect and learn about the individual differences of their peers, particularly regarding culture, race, religion, and socio-economic background.
   g. To further the mission of the Ursuline School by involving its students in a program which addresses societal issues of concern to adolescents and devises ways to help them meet their own needs and the needs of their peers.

Program Activities:
   a. On a weekly basis, time is allocated for meetings. At this time, members of the faculty are trained to teach listening, attending, and responding skills to students wishing to become peer counselors. Weekly assignments are given to the students, who may gain three school credits for completing the program.
   b. Once trained, these counselors facilitate discussion groups with students from grade 10.
   c. Topics covered in the discussion groups have included: goal-setting and accountability; self-esteem; relationships with peers and family; substance abuse; eating disorders; conflict and racial issues; responsibility for behavior/

decision-making; risk-taking; teen pregnancy, sexual behavior; AIDS; date rape; and sexual, psychological and physical abuse.

d. Students are encouraged to be involved in community agencies, and when appropriate, professionals from these agencies are invited to give presentations on specific topics.

Implementing the Program:
  a. Selected faculty need to commit to working on a regular basis with the students in training.
  b. The faculty involved needs extensive training and support.
  c. The school community needs to commit resources, including time and financial support to the program.
  d. Regular evaluations are helpful indicators to gauge progress.

Matignon Catholic High School, Cambridge, MA

Matignon is a coeducational high school owned and operated by the Archdiocese of Boston which enrolls 600 students. The school seeks the integration of new students into the spirit and mission of Matignon Catholic.

Program Focus: New Student /Parent Integration Program seeks to implement the mission goal of creating an environment in which Christian moral and social values provide the basis for the development of student identity, self-worth, and awareness of others. Through an organized program of activities, forums, and opportunities for service,(student-led for students and by the parent organization for parents) students and parents have become more actively involved in extracurricular activities, have developed greater leadership and social skills, and have fostered collaboration among different groups within the school community.

Program Goals:
  a. To make students more aware and responsive to the needs of others;
  b. To help students to fulfill their personal, spiritual, moral, and civic responsibilities;

c. To help the entire community to be clear about the school's mission as a Catholic school community and to provide opportunities for reflection on a regular basis;

d. To orient and integrate, as fully as possible, those new to the school community as to the mission and goals of Matignon Catholic High School.

Program Activities:

a. Members of the adult community of the school provide opportunities for the students, beginning with seniors, to develop leadership skills. This begins in the summer when two evening planning meetings take place. Student leaders in attendance brainstorm the activities and experiences they will provide for the new students.

b. Each member of this core group is responsible for contacting four or five more seniors for the team.

c. Team members write to all new students inviting them to attend two events in September, a morning orientation program conducted by seniors and an evening program for new students and their parents.

d. Team members also invite faculty to be involved and lend their time to attending functions and giving input into the program.

e. Name tags, posters, and activity worksheets are all prepared by the team, so that the welcoming activities will be inclusive, casual, and effective.

f. Follow-up experiences, including a freshman retreat and regular meetings after school for older new students with veteran students keep connections active throughout the students' first year at the school.

Implementing the Program:

a. Adult Training: The administrators need to ask for faculty volunteers to brainstorm student needs, design and evaluate training activities for student leaders and work closely with student leaders to assure that program goals are being followed

b. Student Training: Student leaders need to "buy into" an investment of their time and talent so that the program goals are reached.

c. Appropriate time and funding needs to be committed to the program.
d. Age-appropriate activities need to be designed to make those new to the school feel welcome.
e. Follow-up is essential, so that the program does not appear to be a "one shot" deal.

Chapter 4

Integrating Mission into the Life of Institutions

–Mary M. Brabeck, Otherine Neisler, Nancy J. Zollers

Children and youth enter today's schools with complex and multiple needs. Of the nation's twelve million children under the age of three, 24% are living in poverty and that number is growing (Dryfoos, 1990). About 50% of the approximately 28 million children and adolescents in this country between the ages of 10 and 17 engage in two or more of the following high-risk behaviors: drug and alcohol abuse; crime and violence; school failure and drop out; unsafe sex and teenage parenting. Approximately 10% or nearly 3 million of America's youth engage in all four behaviors (Lerner, R., 1996). Dramatic alterations in family composition and stability, inadequate housing, and violence in neighborhoods, affect the ability of our nation's children and youth to learn.

Many professionals in the fields of medicine, education, social services, and law are concluding that they must collaborate in order to address the complex needs of children, youth, and families (American Bar Association, 1993; American Academy of Pediatrics, 1994). However, most of these professionals have been trained in isolation from other professionals. Lawyers seldom work with teachers; nurses do not collaborate with social workers; psychologists and social workers often work in isolation and, sometimes, competition with each other. At Boston College we are developing a new collaborative model of working across professions to address the complex health, legal, human services, and educational needs of children, youth, and families. We are finding that to succeed, we must collectively claim a mission and integrate it into the life of the university and our individual efforts.

Collaborative Efforts within Boston College: Toward a Mission of Service

For the past four years the Boston College School of Education, Law School, Graduate School of Social Work, School of Nursing, Carroll School of Management and the College of Arts and Sciences have been working collaboratively in four overlapping and integrated efforts. In our educational effort, we are drawing from the knowledge bases of our diverse professions and disciplines to design curricula that will prepare professionals to work more effectively with children, families, and communities. Our community outreach effort creates partnerships with local schools, clinics, hospitals, and community agencies. Our scholarship effort builds collaborative, co-learning research agendas that address questions designed by community members (as opposed to university faculty). Finally, reflecting on our collaborative research and service delivery, we are developing policy statements to inform federal and local governments. Our efforts move the faculty out of the ivory tower of the university and into the real world of local schools and communities in ways that are consonant with the mission of Boston College.

Boston College, a Jesuit University, founded in 1863 to provide a Catholic liberal arts education for immigrants, has had a long standing commitment to the action-knowledge link and an institutional identity marked by an obligation to serve others (Byrne, 1995). We have carried this service orientation into our efforts at joining thought and action through interprofessional collaboration. We have organized and maintained a monthly faculty seminar to expand our knowledge of interprofessional collaboration, revised aspects of professional preparation programs, and altered curriculum to better reflect the knowledge bases of the diverse professions engaged in our discussions. We have created faculty and student work teams who go to schools and community agencies and work collaboratively. We have formed panels and written papers that describe our efforts and how this work achieves the mission of Boston College (Brabeck, M., Cawthorne, J., Cochran-Smith, M., Gaspard, N., Hurd-Green, C., Kenny, M., Krawczyk, R., Lowery, C., Lykes, M. B., Minuskin, A. D., Mooney, J., Ross, C., Savage, J., Soifer, A., Smyer, M., Sparks, E., Tourse, R., Turillo, R. M., Waddock, S., Walsh, M. E., & Zollers, N., in press; Brabeck, M., Walsh, M., Kenny, M. & Comilang, K., in press; Walsh, M., Bellanca, J., Brown, K., Chastenay, M. & Kabadian, M., 1996).

Rev. J. Donald Monan, S.J., Chancellor of Boston College, and past President, described the mission of the University, which is rooted in Ignatian spirituality, as resting "not in a particular virtue or speculative principle but in the motive or intention of service - namely, in all things to better serve the Lord out of passionate love (Monan, J. D., 1991, p. 13). More recently, Rev. William P. Leahy, S.J., current President of Boston College, stated in his inaugural address that Boston College must "develop appropriate responses to the issues of justice, faith, and fairness and in this way serve the common good" (Leahy, 1996, p. 30). The Jesuit challenge, to find God in all things, has been at the core of the Boston College mission and is the foundation on which our interprofessional collaborative work rests. If faculty and students are to find God in all things, the university may not be separate from the world; rather, we must be engaged in it. We must encircle the lives of the children and youth and families most at risk in today's society and we must enlarge our circle of community to contain them.

The circle is the metaphor for our work at Boston College. We claim a holistic approach which views the individual family and

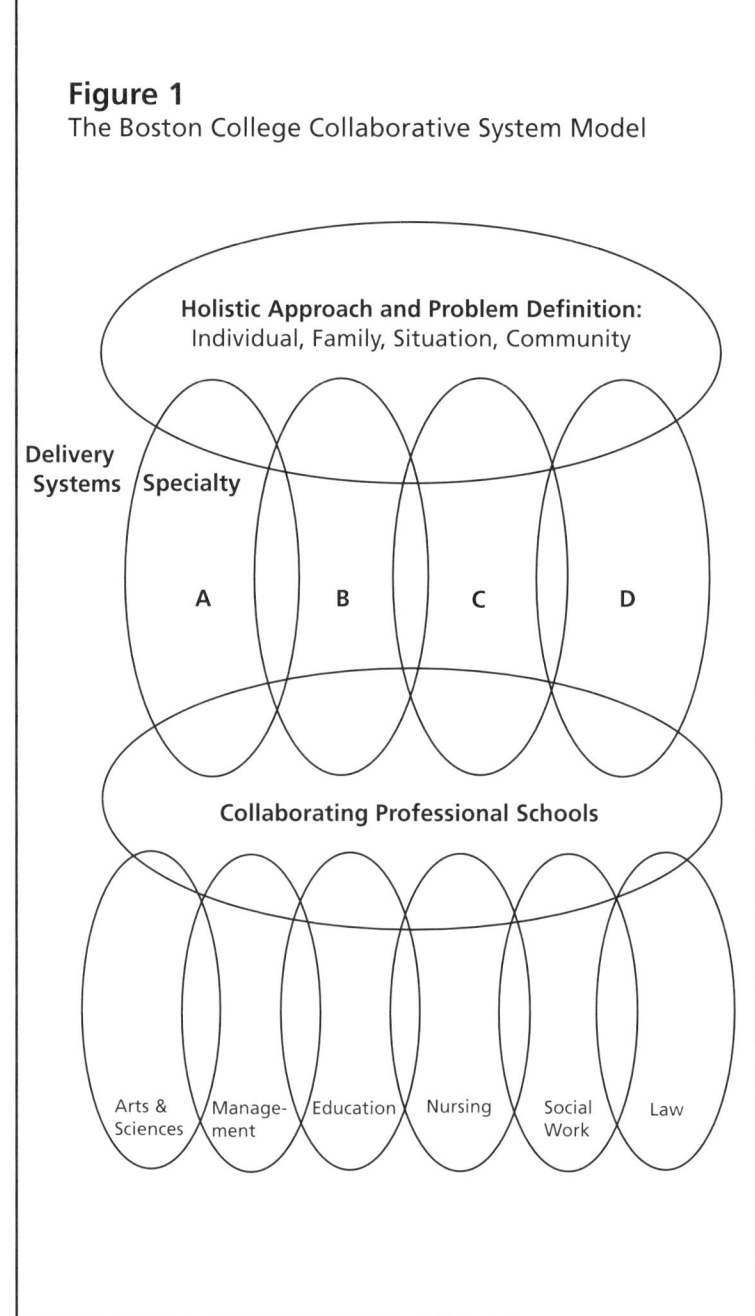

community from multiple and inter-related bio-psycho-social perspectives that require collaboration of professionals from law, psychology, education, health, and social services. Our model, illustrated in Figure 1, involves overlapping circles that reflect collaboration among the professional schools and College of Arts and Sciences and in co-operation with delivery systems such as schools and clinics (Waddock, S., 1996). When we first began our collaborations, we worked independently in isolated circles. Now our circles are beginning to overlap. As we learn more from working as a team, the borders of our independent fields have blurred, though not disappeared. No one of us can do the entire (or even large segments) of the job alone, but our team efforts bring our multiple expertises to any one case. The information flows along a spiral as we address the multiple needs of the student, and students feel less like they are being passed from one place to another, from one professional to the next.

The concept within the Catholic tradition that most vividly symbolizes our circle of community is the mystical body of Christ. This concept embodies the belief that we are all spiritually united, rooted together in a common bond, a community of love. All the good which anyone of us does enhances all members of the community. All the pain which any one of us suffers is suffered throughout the mystical body of Christ. This concept both supports and challenges us. It supports us in our recognition that working collaboratively makes us stronger, and more capable of addressing the complex needs of children, youth, and families. It challenges us in our acknowledgment that we have a responsibility to improve the life chances of the most unfortunate members of our enlarged community circle.

Efforts to create collaborative partnerships across professions and with communities is a return to an earlier outreach mission of higher education. According to Ernest Boyer, the late historian of higher education, the goal in previous years "was not only to *serve* society but *reshape it*" (Boyer, 1990, p. 6). The conviction that higher education has a moral obligation to improve society calls upon all universities to join in partnerships with communities to solve the problems that community members and agencies define. In a special way, it calls upon Catholic universities whose mission is one of service. Father Leahy noted that nearly 30 years ago Riesman and Jencks wrote, "There is yet no university that manages to fuse academic professionalism with concern for questions of ultimate social and moral importance" and called on Boston College to be the counter-cultural university that addresses the eternal questions through "lives illuminated by faith discovery and service" (Leahy, 1996, p. 30). This is at the heart of the social justice mission at Boston College.

Social Justice and the Mission of the School of Education

The Jesuit character of the university, inspired by the order's self-understanding of social justice through its General Congregations and Superior General, entails a preferential option for the poor and an elimination of social, economic, and political structures that oppress people. This is the theological and ethical foundation on which the mission of the Boston College School of Education (SOE) is being articulated.

While the social justice mission is central to the work of many SOE and university-wide faculty, we have come to understand that social justice has many meanings. The multiple meanings have become a subject of weekly dialogue among the teacher education faculty in the School of Education. The entire teacher education faculty, including elementary, secondary, and special education, agreed to work toward understanding each other's and their own perspectives on social justice.

Dialogue across a diverse group of faculty members about university mission is complex and difficult work. We decided to engage in this work, because we are interested in 1) how our mission of social justice is defined by each of us, 2) whether we can agree on some common understandings of social justice, and 3) how we envision incorporating mission into our work as teachers, advisors, and researchers. If these conversations are successful among teacher education faculty, we will have created a teacher education program that integrates mission into the work we do, including the research questions we ask, the decisions we make, the plans we formulate, and the priorities we set.

With support from School of Education administrators, our goal is to infuse the social justice values into the School of Education mission. Such an effort is also occurring at the university level.

Integrating mission into the life of the school requires a deliberate dialogue to articulate a mission of service that promotes social justice. Consistent with the University mission, (Advancing the Legacy, 1996) faculty and staff have examined the mission of Boston College and the distinctive contribution our School of Education can make to society. Our discussion of how the mission is actualized in the work of faculty, staff, and students has led us to develop a shared language, essential for institutional change. Faculty and administrators speak of "preparing contemplative activists" by joining reflection and action, the thinking and doing, in a way that will further the Ignation mission to serve others and to find God in all things.

The emerging teacher education, school, and university missions are affecting our practice in schools and communities. Collaborative work in the community and in the schools, off campus and shoulder to shoulder with our neighbors, provides the faculty with clear opportunities to work with community members, children, and families to achieve social justice. While university teaching, advising young students, and scholarly research are complex enough to provide opportunities to live this mission, the outreach scholarship which faculty engage in offers stark and multiple opportunities for work with growing, hurting, or puzzled children. Our work in Boston public schools has been in a community which has many needs and great hope. There are many children who are homeless, abused, failing in school, scared, or ignored. There are also children and families who are growing up healthy and bright. Boston is a community of resilient children, with wonderful cultural and language diversity. In both the families in pain and the children of hope, we are finding God, and working to achieve social justice through our outreach with, and service in, the schools.

Challenges and Barriers to a Mission of Collaboration for Social Justice for a University.

There are a number of challenges and barriers to this work and identifying them is critical to the development of mission. Among the challenges that we have identified, the most significant are the ones within each of us. Each of us was educated in a model of autonomy and independence and have little experience with interprofessional collaboration. We have our professional identifies and these identities carry hierarchical valuing; e.g. teachers and lawyers do not have the same status. We all have the normal apprehension about exposing the limits of our knowledge, skills, and ability. Our biggest challenge has been to learn to trust each other. We continually learn that if we can keep focused on the mission of our work, i.e., to improve the lives of children, youth and families, we can make progress. There are many barriers to keeping that focus including our language.

Naming is powerful when it describes or locates a problem. We had, for example, different opinions about the first sentence of this article, and discussed these different beginnings: "Children come to school faced with navigating the complex and multiple problems of our culture," or "Children come to school with complex and multiple needs," or "Children come to school with complex and multiple problems." Each of these sentences suggests a different approach to working with children in schools. Is the root of the problem in the children's behavior or in the society which does not provide adequately for these children? We recognize that these are not merely semantic problems and we place our language and that of our students as a central focus of our critical analysis. We hope to reveal and clarify the values and assumptions which direct the approaches to the work we collaboratively pursue.

Power is inherent in naming one's self, one's problem, or one's need, or those of others. Consider, for example, that at one multicultural curriculum discussion the moderator (an African American female who refers to herself as such but who also often calls herself Black) referred to groups as Black and White. A White female referred to herself as Anglo and a White male used the term European American. Another White male wanted the group to adopt a common term to be used by all. We decided to try to continue our conversations using the preferred terms for each person. Rather than becoming entwined in arguments about political correctness, we felt this was empowering to all and any compromise would have a reverse affect.

Definitions also hamper our progress. The word "confidentiality" has, for example, many meanings and operational definitions.

When lawyers on our teams talk to students, those conversations are legally protected as privileged communication. Unless a student gives his or her consent, those conversations are not shared with any others on the professional team. Yet, if a students tells certain information (e.g., reveals sexual abuse) to a teacher, that teacher is required by law to make a referral. Counselors, therapists, and nurses all face similar predicaments. It is, therefore, possible for members of a team of six professionals to have different information about a child and be unable to communicate that information to each other. Conflicts have arisen when a teacher makes a referral to another professional and is left out of the information and counseling process because of confidentiality. Our work is leading us to consider carefully policy concerning information flow in the schools.

While we all claim to embrace social justice in our work, our divergent understandings of social justice lead us to envision our mission from several different perspectives. One of the authors of this article believes, for example, that social justice depends on changing American values and mores. She sees the "culture of greed" and the huge disparity of income distribution as the root of all of our problems; that variation in values regarding sexual practice, pregnancy, abortion, welfare, the elderly, and downsizing create a climate that is nearly impossible to change in the schools. She believes that we can only address the symptoms but never cure the illness through our integrated services work. Others in SOE believe that our work should be to change the existing structures by working within them. They point to students who are able to create meaningful lives within today's complex world, and urge us to struggle toward both individual and structural transformation.

Recognizing that the root of the problem may be beyond the scope of our interprofessional team, our mission lead us three years ago to make changes in our university curricula. In the School of Education we added a required course called "The Social Contexts of Education" at the graduate level and "The Child and Society" at the undergraduate level. The latter course educates students about the realities of social problems that impact student learning and development. This course also fulfills a new university core undergraduate requirement that all students at Boston College take at least one three credit course that addresses issues of human diversity. Other courses also address social justice issues in accord with our mission; for example, one member of our faculty held a three credit seminar designed to help our doctoral students understand and debunk the suppositions presented in *The Bell Curve* (Hernstein & Murray, 1994). In many courses we encourage our students to become active in policy-making agencies in their communities and states and at the federal level.

The Boston College-Boston Schools Collaborative Efforts

While we have a great deal to learn about collaboration, we are trying to work in mutually supportive and respectful partnerships between the university and the schools, and we are learning to collaboratively deliver services in the schools and agencies. Our collaborative model assumes interdependence among individuals, organizations, and even whole systems, and our institutional mission and values provide a context essential for our ongoing commitment to the work.

We have developed integrated services/interprofessional collaboration teams within four inner-city Boston schools in a neighborhood community. While we have worked in two elementary schools, a middle school, and a high school, we focus here first on the high school and later on one of the elementary schools to provide some examples of our work and how our mission informs our work.

The high school serves approximately 1200 students from working class and low-income families. The diverse student body includes Hispanic, African American, Asian American, Caribbean American, and some Eastern European students. Many students are first-or second-generation immigrants. The faculty is predominately white male and female with a small number of Black, Asian, and Hispanic teachers. Built in the late 1890s the building looks somewhat like a castle, with high ceilings, large windows, and is chronically in need of repairs and renovations. After being on probation because of inadequate facilities, including an inadequate library, the high school has recently regained its accreditation.

Community agencies, businesses and universities are working with the school administration, staff and faculty. Social service agency support is coordinated by the student support teams which develop action plans to address the needs of students. A local hospital works with the school in a health careers cluster, through which we train students for part-time work in the hospital. Many of these students are hired permanently after graduation. Our efforts are coordinated by the headmaster who yearly holds a planning session to develop with deans and faculty, a strategic plan that will facilitate greater exchange of information, and coordination of efforts.

Our faculty and students entered the high school in many different ways. Counseling, guidance, and nursing interns began by participating in the student support teams with the school personnel. Student teachers have been placed throughout the school in one of their three professional placements. We are in the second year of a legal services program in which law students and a law faculty member provide free legal and referral services to the high school students. Law students also teach "Youth and the Law" sessions in the tenth grade civics class.

Opportunities for collaboration also arise out of individual student or faculty interests which pose different challenges and opportunities. A doctoral student is working with parents to develop strategies for greater parental involvement. She is also testing a parent guidebook developed by the Urban League, which houses its Department of Education in our School of Education. A master's student is working with students to determine what support services they want from the school and from their parents. His work is supported by a special education inclusion grant and by the Urban League, Department of Education.

We are also collaborating in research. University-based research must be negotiated with and to the degree possible "owned" by school personnel, and directly benefit the schools; for example, Neisler's research on the sociopolitical attitude development of adolescents evolved from her observation and participation in social studies classes (Neisler, 1994). Neisler found that students were expressing attitudes about society, politics, and each other but were not called upon to understand or examine their assumptions, their logic, or any related factual information. Teachers at the high school are using Neisler's research to modify their instruction.

In addition, one faculty member wrote a partnership grant with the special education coordinator to work with the social studies and the ninth grade cluster teachers on inclusion of special-needs students in the regular classroom. We are in the second year of funding of that grant. Our efforts to engage in outreach to an elementary school that was moving toward inclusion formed the basis for our inclusion grant at the high school. The elementary school is described next.

Working Within A Context of Inclusion: The Elementary School

There is always a context within which we do our interprofessional work that derives from the culture, habits, and history of the schools and community, and the goals and mission of the schools that we enter. Our work with an elementary school that is inclusive, illustrates how collaborators bring multiple perspectives to work on common goals and development of a joint mission.

The principal of the elementary school within which we are working, is in her fourth year of creating an inclusion school. She sees the exclusion of children from regular classes into any pull-out models of special services as extremely problematic. For her it is a matter of social justice that everyone should be included in the regular class. She developed a model in which all special teachers who formerly had small classes in special education or remedial reading became classroom teachers in her building. This allowed her to achieve a class size for every teacher of 15-18 children, down from 30 or more. In this urban elementary school, there were so many children with language, learning and behavior needs that the process of "sorting out" who was in need of special education became nonsensical. The small class size was designed to allow a more individualized approach to the classroom.

Through weekly meetings of an interprofessional support team consisting of BC faculty and school personnel, we address the needs of students who are at risk. The team includes the classroom teacher, school- and community-based professionals and university faculty. As we strategized with school staff about children in serious trouble academically, emotionally, or socially, we came to value the voices from diverse professionals. Interprofessional collaboration has the benefit of obtaining different perspectives on the social contexts in which we work. As we worked collaboratively, we had the opportunity to understand that the inclusion model that the principal developed, based on notions of fairness and good pedagogy, was perceived in many ways: for some teachers, the idea of including everyone was frightening and made them question their own training and capabilities; for others, this model called into question their basic assumptions that specialists know more and can do different things for children; still others saw inclusion as increasing their teaching burdens; and yet others questioned whether inclusion in a regular classroom was adequately meeting the needs of the targeted students.

Inclusion allows a student the right to an appropriate education in regular classes with necessary services and supports. That right is violated when the supports and services are not available. Therefore, in the same school that made inclusion seem logical because of the large number of children in need, efforts at inclusion were thwarted because there were few resources to make it work smoothly. Working with too few resources and not enough support is a daily struggle, with or without one more complicated child.

Like all urban teachers, these teachers were asked to do more with less. Inclusion often takes more teacher time to accomplish and often requires teachers to re-evaluate their current practices. This is one more obligation in an under-funded school. However, when the principal designed her inclusive school, she did not intend to dump children in any classroom without regard to what they needed to learn. She understood that inclusion means individualizing a common curriculum so everyone meets high standards of learning.

The goal of inclusion, when implemented in a poor school district with a faculty with a wide range of competence and commitment, allowed the school staff to talk about this mission and challenge it for the first time (Hilliard, A., 1988). Having the university present encouraged the discussion which revealed these multiple perspectives. As this example illustrates, our collaborative work in schools has potential to illuminate school practices that require multiple perspectives to move toward a common goal. Our work in schools also helps bridge the theory-practice gap by allowing theorists to redefine theory for the practitioners and practitioners to react to the theoretical constructs out of their classroom experience.

Challenges and Complexities to University–School Collaboration

The challenge and complexities of interprofessional work was illustrated recently at a meeting of students who have a practicum in the school. Boston College student teachers, student counselors, student nurses, and student social workers met, as they routinely do, to discuss their work in the schools. A student from counseling psychology, who meets with small groups of children in the school to support and listen to them, asked how to handle the fact that she did not want the stories that were told "in group" to be retold back in the classroom. She was concerned about confidentiality and about maintaining openness and trust in the group. The student teacher was troubled that children might be sharing private stories that could be repeated. She also wondered if the families fully understood what these groups were, and questioned the value of taking children out of the classroom during academic time. A social work student thought the groups were very valuable to teach social skills the students badly needed. She saw them as skill building groups, not counseling groups. Another student wondered what the impact was on the students when it was decided that they should go to group. She found some children reluctant to come with her when she arrived in class. Each Boston College student saw the work very differently from his or her professional perspective, and each perspective broadened the counseling student's understanding of the complexities of her work.

We see our work as evolutionary, defined by the direction the public school sets and influenced by our Jesuit university and School of Education missions. At times this leads to multiple and conflicting pressures. We find when the school-university relationship develops there is no end to the requests we receive from schools. Urban schools have very limited resources and we become a powerful addition to their few resources. We are asked for student teachers, student counselors, student lawyers, student social workers, and student nurses. We are asked for books, to do workshops, to find literature, to gather information, and to judge the science fair. We are asked to write grants, meet school officials, talk with parents. A university faculty could easily become drained by agreeing to the multiple requests of schools and communities. We could provide student teachers and tutors to teach use of the computers as well as literacy and second language acquisition and other professionals; we could distribute materials and conduct seminars about nutrition, drug use, violence prevention, or parenting skills; we could extend the legal services clinic to the parents of students; and provide nursing care, medical referrals, and social services. Setting priorities with the school is crucial to preventing burnout. Keeping our mission clearly in mind helps us make difficult decisions about where and how to use our human and material resources.

In order to accomplish our social justice mission to find God in the community, the traditional university role has to be turned on its head. To work together as partners the community needs to know that this collaboration would not be a traditional university relationship. Those traditional relationships often leave communities distrustful of our motives and our commitments. Boston College is dedicated to help meet the communities needs, not merely the research needs of the university. We are in the schools every week to demonstrate that we are partners in tackling the everyday issues that the community faces. Using the school's agenda, working together often and over the long haul has resulted in an extraordinary collaboration built on trust. The result has been that our interprofessional work in the real world of schools has had important outcomes for both the schools and the university.

Results for the University

For the university faculty the outcomes have been many. We have the opportunity to feel exhilarated at living an activist life with the community, as its members struggle to improve their lives. This mission, described earlier, feels to us like good work, for some it is God's work. Second, our classes and our curriculum are profoundly and forever changed. We now teach very differently, incorporating what we know from our community work and knowing more clearly how our students must be prepared for their work in the future.

Our students might be the most fortunate of us all. They were able to join our interprofessional team in their schools and they observed their professors collaborating with each other and with the community professionals. They have been prepared in a new paradigm of collaboration among the professionals concerned with children and families at Boston College through their work in the schools.

Results for the Community

The community and the schools in which we work should speak to the results for them with their own voice, but our close partnership allows us to highlight a few outcomes as we see them. While no single activity can eradicate the conditions of poverty and school failure in urban centers, the Boston College partnership with the urban schools had direct and important impacts on many children and their families. In addition, the community professionals with whom we worked learned from us, as we learned from them. University faculty brought different perspectives, energy, and ideas to the work in the schools. Third, the school met in support teams to discuss children and families every week. The chaos of urban schools easily interferes with extraordinary activities, like meeting to problem solve about children in trouble, as important as those activities might be. The fact that the team from the university was coming to the school each week solidified opportunities to discuss children needing attention, resources, etc., and possible solutions as we saw them.

Our impact has been so positive that the headmaster of the High School recently spoke to a group meeting of twenty Boston College faculty and staff who work in her school. During the meeting she identified her concerns about the need for the ninth grade students to set goals and to develop strategies for their attainment, and said she hoped that we can form an interprofessional group to further support the ninth grade cluster. The principal at the elementary school has recently joined us in the fourth year of funded work on inclusion. The school, community, and university have recently collaborated to seek funding for an extended services school to address the needs of children and families after and before school hours.

We will continue to call on the Catholic tradition of social justice for strength, guidance and sustained commitment to our individual and collective work. We believe that the Boston College story of integrating mission into the life of the university is a story that has lessons for Catholic schools that attempt to draw on their mission, so as to better serve the complex needs of children, youth, and families.

The university's outreach scholarship and the Catholic character of Boston College, suggests a link between Boston College's collaborative service mission and a network of Catholic schools. Through the Selected Programs in Catholic Education (SPICE) the university provides a forum for practitioners to learn from practitioners, with the opportunities for reflection within the academy. Boston College is uniquely poised to identify and assess successful programs, and uniquely able to provide a forum in which these programs are shared through conferences on campus and through publications. Our efforts to realize our mission through interprofessional collaboration in service to urban children in public schools provides one such example.

References

Brabeck, M., Walsh, M., Kenny, M. & Comilang, K. (In press). Interprofessional collaboration for children and families: Opportunities for Counseling Psychology in the Twenty-First Century. *The Counseling Psychologist*.

Byrne, P. (1995). Paradigms of Justice and Love. *Conversations*. National Center on Jesuit Higher Education. St. Louis, MO.

Dryfoos, J. G. (1990). *Adolescents at risk: Prevalence and Prevention*. New York: Oxford University.

Hernstein, R.J. & Murray, C. (1994). *The Bell Curve*. New York: Free Press.

Hilliard, A. (1988). "Public Support for Successful Instructional Practices for At-Risk Students." In *School Success for Students at Risk*. San Diego, CA: Harcourt Brace Javonovich.

Leahy, W. (1996) Rededication: The Inaugural address. *Boston College Magazine*, Fall.

Lerner, R. M. (1995). *America's Youth in Crisis: Challenges and Options for Programs and Policies*. Thousand Oaks, CA: Sage.

Monan, J. D. (l991). From Palaces to Ghettos, A Jesuit Legacy of Action and Devotion, *Boston Globe*, April 22, p. 13.

Neisler, O.J. (1994). I*nside Castleton High School: Development of Secondary Student's Sociopolitical Attitudes*. Unpublished dissertation: Syracuse University.

Waddock, S. (1996). *An Emerging Model of Integrated Services and Interprofessional Collaboration: Working Together for Community Welfare*. Paper presented at the Academy of Management Annual Meeting.

Walsh, M., Bellanca, J. Brown, K., Chastenay, M. & Kabadian, M. (l996). *Integrated Services/Interprofessional Collaoration and Related Areas*. Unpublished document, Boston College, Chestnut Hill, MA.

Postscript

A short summary of this work was published in *Momentum*. The work described here is due to the efforts of many faculty at Boston College and we acknowledge their role and contribution. The work has been funded by the Massachusetts Department of Education, the DeWitt-Wallace Reader's Digest Foundation through the National Center for Social Work and Education Collaboration at Fordham University, the U.S. Office of Education (Fund for the Improvement of Post Secondary Education; Patricia Roberts Harris Grant), and Philip Morris Companies Inc.

Chapter 5

Mission & Catholic Education: Theological Perspectives

–Margaret Eletta Guider, OSF

As this 1996 S.P.I.C.E. conference draws to a close, I am mindful of the fact that as participants you have been challenged and encouraged by the proceedings of the past few days. As I understand the task entrusted to me by the organizers of today's program, the purpose of my being here is not to provide you with more information, but rather to focus on some other objectives such as inspiration, integration, affirmation, and perhaps a bit of agitation as well. Essentially, my presentation is a theological reflection on mission and Catholic education. The outline for this reflection includes seven brief considerations of selected themes which I believe to be foundational for a

theology of mission. These themes include:
1. Participating in God's Mission
2. Pondering Our Experiences of Amazement and Fear
3. Tending the Bridges of Life
4. Rethinking Our Understanding of the Incarnation
5. Following the Example of Jesus
6. Daring to Ask "Why the Child is Crying?"
7. Reimagining the Future as the Advent of the Not Yet

I think it is reasonable to assume that those of us gathered together today share a common conviction that God is doing something new in and through Catholic education. The question is: How do we as Catholic educators and administrators perceive God's action in our own lives and throughout the world?

Participating in God's Mission

In my effort to put forth a few thoughts about some of the ways in which our understanding of Christian mission may be best integrated into the life of Catholic educational institutions, I would like to begin by reflecting upon how we as Catholic educators and administrators understand our participation in God's mission - individually and collectively. My objective here is not to focus on what we are doing or should be doing in order to accomplish *our mission*, but rather on how we are participating in *God's mission*. This mission, described in the Gospels as the Reign of God is more than a 'dream worth having,' it is a reality worth sharing.'

During the past several years, I have attended a number of educational conferences that have focused on the theme of mission. If I were asked to capture the essence and atmosphere of many of these meetings by way of a pithy description, I would offer the following title: **Presumption** *and* **Despair**: *the* **Problem** *of Being Sent for Mission*. I highlight presumption because of a generalized tendency to project on to Catholic education the image of having all the answers. I highlight despair because so many Catholic educators feel under siege - economically, culturally, professionally, legally, socially, politically, and even ecclesiastically. All too often, discussions focusing on mission end up serving as a forum for giving expression to accolades or anxieties about what we have done or what we have failed to do. In such discussions, mission is seen more as a problem than a mystery. For this reason, I would like to turn attention away from experiences of presumption or despair associated with the problem of mission, so as to focus attention on our experiences of amazement and fear when the mystery of being gathered for mission reminds us of our responsibility for a reality worth sharing.

Unquestionably, the times in which we live are demanding something different from us, something new, something unfamiliar. Whether by invitation, force, or serendipity, we find ourselves in the midst of experiences that are potentially as unsettling as they are transformative. Yet, how do we make meaning out of what is happening to each of us, to some of us, and to all of us? How do we render an accounting of these movements in life that lead us from presumption to fear, from despair to amazement, from being sent to being gathered, from problem to mystery? Amazed and fearful, how do we as Catholic educators and administrators, serving traditionally Catholic institutions, enter into the mystery of being gathered to participate in God's mission? How do we respond to this ongoing call to bear witness to the Reign of God?

Pondering Our Experiences of Amazement and Fear

As I mentioned early on, discussions of mission embedded in presumption or despair are often bound to be reflections on what has been or what might have been. Nostalgia or amnesia, when combined with presumption or despair, have a way of harnessing our imaginations in ways that prevent us from exploring with open minds and open hearts what could be or what is yet to be.

I would like to argue that as educators, committed to a gospel vision of life, the quality of our participation in God's mission is contingent upon our willingness to move beyond presumption or despair. Moreover, I contend that it is dependent upon the degree to which we allow our experiences of amazement and fear to teach us something about Jesus, about His mission, about those who followed Him and the risk of discipleship. I think the following excerpts from Mark's Gospel speak for themselves.

As you listen to these passages, I invite you to consider the ways in which they shed light on some of your own experiences, feelings, and insights as teachers, as learners, as disciples, and as imitators of Christ. [Cf. Mark 1:22; 1:27; 2:12; 4:41; 4:40; 5:15; 5:17; 5:21; 5:23; 5:36; 5:43; 6:3; 6:50; 6:51; 7:37; 9:6; 9:32; 10:26; 10:32; 11:18; 11:32; 12:12; 12:17; 16:5; 16:8].

These excerpts from Mark's Gospel illustrate that fear is not only an indicator of an absence of faith, but an indicator of faith that is being recomposed. Amazement is not only an indicator of a lack of understanding, but an indicator of relationships that are being reoriented. I would like to characterize these two experiences of fear and amazement as central to the experience of what it means to participate in God's mission. In a way, these two experiences signal change and uncertainty. They alert us to the ongoing process of transformation. To remember our own experiences of fear and amazement is to remind ourselves of those transformative moments in our own lives that may be best described as "bridge experiences."

Tending the Bridges of Life

As individuals we are all too familiar with the rigors and ambiguities of human growth and development. In every crossing-over experience of our own lives, we have known what it feels like to be afraid or to be amazed. Every bridge we cross attunes us to the myriad ways in which our inner structures as human persons are broken down, refashioned, and enlarged. We have known the experience of not being able to understand or to speak, until we are able to make meaning of what has happened to us. Through reflection on our own processes of transformation, we recognize the importance and significance of those who have served as the bridge tenders in our lives. We remember those who guaranteed the moorings of the bridges that made possible our own passage from unknowing to knowing.

As Catholic educators, I believe our distinctive call as participants in God's mission may be to serve as "bridge-tenders" for others so as to ensure that the metaphorical bridges of their lives may be securely anchored on both sides. Inasmuch as the process of education is predicated on experiences of fear and amazement and, ultimately, of crossing over, we are the ones to whom others look for assurance that the process of transformation is worthy of trust, that the process of evolution is in the plan of creation, and that these processes are of God. As bridge tenders, our task is to encourage those who arrive at the bridges of their lives to risk "crossing over." As bridge tenders, our responsibility is to welcome and support those who reach the threshold of the other side, fearful, amazed, and uncertain about whether or not they have the courage to leave the bridge and step into a new way of being in the world. As their faith in God, themselves, and others is recomposed and the relationships of their lives are reoriented, we become witnesses to God's grace at work in their lives as well as our own. Regardless of their age or abilities, we are at once privileged and pained to be part of 'a growth observed' as those who call us teacher endeavor to make meaning of who they are and who they are becoming.

Rethinking Our Understanding of the Incarnation

During the past few days, you have had an opportunity to share with one another your experiences of God's presence and action in your lives as Catholic educators. But who exactly is this God who calls you to participate in mission? Who is this God who is closer to you than you are to yourselves? I pose these questions as a way of emphasizing that they are not the private domain of theologians. Inasmuch as these questions emerge whenever and wherever Christians try to make meaning of God's mission as well as their own, they belong to all of us. To put it more precisely, behind each of these questions rests the foundational question of our faith. The question is simply this: Why did God become human?

Though I recognize the fact that throughout the centuries there have been many attempts to answer this question, I think it continues to merit our consideration. Why did God become human? To save us? To be with us? As Catholic educators, it is not enough for us to *answer* this question, we also must learn to *live* with it. If we are to take seriously the Christian task of imitating Christ, we need to be clear about who we are imitating and why.

Historically speaking, our understanding is informed and influenced by the preferred theological opinion of the Christian tradition, namely, that God became human to redeem us from our sins. Unquestionably, this has been handed down as the preferred opinion. I would like, however, to underscore the fact that, while *not* the preferred theological opinion, it is no less orthodox to believe that, moved by love and a desire to be one with all creation, God's first intention was to be one with us. As a good Franciscan, I would be remiss if I did not highlight this point. Imagine if we were to live our lives in such a way that our imitation of Christ continually affirmed that God's first intention in becoming human was born out of love and the desire to be one with us, to be God-with-us.

As Catholic educators, committed to teaching as Jesus taught, we do well to remember that Jesus invites the disciples to participate in God's mission when he speaks the words, "Follow me" (Mk 2:14). Implicit in this call to mission is, however, the invitation, "Come be present with me–and with others." In responding to this call, we ground our understanding of mission in a theology of presence that recognizes God's action in our world, not only as the definitive solution to the problem of evil and sin, but as the definitive revelation of the mystery of God's love. To come to terms with this call as Catholic educators and administrators is to understand more fully our vocation in the world as witnesses, not only to God's liberating grace, but of God's loving presence.

Following the Example of Jesus

A few years ago, a film was made about a small community of French Huguenots that hid Jews from the Nazi soldiers during World War II. I found it striking that while the interviewer was trying to make heroes and heroines out of these individuals, constructing them as extraordinary exemplars of altruism, the individuals' self-perception was one of ordinariness, of doing only what the Gospel asked them to do. In their minds, they had done nothing beyond the ordinary. In a book entitled *The Altruistic Personality* (Olner, S. & Olner, P., 1988), this finding was reconfirmed. Repeatedly, individuals identified by others as exceptional or extraordinary people, did not see themselves as anything but average and quite ordinary, simply doing what needed to be done.

For those of you who are familiar with the literature on religious life and prophetic action, I believe an anecdote about a very wise senior sister merits some consideration. Upon listening to a number of sisters talk about prophetic action as resettling refugees, assisting persons with serious disabilities, caring for persons who are dying, ministering to people in correctional centers, and defending the rights of the homeless, she tentatively asked those assembled, "Why is this prophetic?" After several people tried to explain, she modestly thanked them for their reflections, and simply said, "Most of my life has been spent in what is now called the ministry of education, a ministry that I have been led to believe falls outside of the category of the so-called prophetic. And perhaps, rightly so. Over the course of fifty-five years of living in the inner city of Chicago, I simply did what I thought anyone in my position would have done. I tried to teach as Jesus taught. I never thought of it as prophecy, I just thought of it as the work of the Gospel."

It goes without saying that the insights disclosed in this anecdote teach us a thing or two about the fidelity and creativity of Catholic educators. When your memories of these days together at the SPICE conference begin to wane and the demands of being gathered for mission are overwhelming, I encourage you to remember this story and to take a moment to read the Parable of the Talents [Matt 25:14-30]. Remember that the message of the parable is that God expects more of all of us than fidelity. The Gospel that we have received has been given to us for more than safe keeping. Regardless of the evaluation standards set by your respective states or your dioceses, the measure of your success are the standards set by the Reign of God. The measures of your success are not about being counted among the most perfect, the most prophetic, or the most extraordinary. It is about continuing to teach as Jesus taught with fidelity and *creativity*, daring to ask the questions that no one else is asking, and courageously providing answers that no one else is expecting.

Daring to Ask "Why the Child is Crying?"

Before proceeding, I invite you to imagine yourself standing in the door way of the room in which you are sitting. Imagine that you are an eight-year-old child. What do you see? What do you remember? What makes an impression? How do you tell the story to another? What would you say? I invite you now to identify an insight that came to you as you engaged in this exercise.

Given the fact that the purpose of this exercise may not be readily apparent to you, allow me to explain my intentions. I have asked you to take the perspective of a child for what I believe to be a very good reason. How easy it is for us to come to a gathering like this and yet never give a thought to what meaning or significance a third of the world's population, our little sisters and brothers, would give to these proceedings.

We live in a world where reports of death threats and assassinations of street children draw our attention to the fact that death squads and vigilantes exterminate children with impunity. Twenty-five years ago, their targets would have been union leaders, journalists, university students, and social workers. On the streets of my own city of Chicago, children are used by gangs to kill other children only to be killed by the gangs themselves. One of the sisters with whom I live recently recounted her experience of being with a young sixteen-year-old mother, who after spending a few hours with her newborn son in the maternity ward of the city hospital, was taken handcuffed and chained at the ankles by police who returned her to a holding cell in the juvenile detention center. Daily the media provides us with images of children who are abandoned and abused, children who are as hungry as they are hostile, children who are living to die, and children who are dying to live. These stories and faces are only the beginning.

In conscience, I cannot help but ask: of what real consequence is a conference such as this for the children of our world (UNICEF, 1995)? And more to the point, of what real significance is this reflection? Do the proceedings of these days hold any potential for challenging the delusions and distortions of the cultures and contexts in which we live and teach? For most of us, the world or worlds in which we live are constructed primarily by adults and for adults. It is we who benefit the most from this world, from these worlds, whether we thrive or merely survive. Yet there is something about the identification of children with the Reign of God [Mark 10:14-15; Lk 9:48] that must capture our imagination in these times, when the greatest counter-cultural activity and gospel witness is a preferential option for children. Among the hard sayings of Jesus, the injunctions against those who scandalize children are unambiguous. Jesus' own admonitions to the apostles who attempted to relegate children to a place of insignificance are sobering. The fact that Jesus repeatedly responds to the immediate needs of children, regardless of who their parents are, should be more than sufficient cause for continuing to participate in God's mission as Catholic educators.

Why is the child crying? Why are the *children* crying? If we do not ask these questions, who will? The fact that our God comes to us as an infant has profound religious and ethical implications for our world. If God-with-us is first a child with us, how far is this world of ours from understanding and responding to the demands of the Reign of God? Of the many miracles Jesus performs, a number of them involve children. There are miracles involving sick children who are returned to good health and dead children who are brought back to life. There are children possessed by demons who are set free. There are hungry children who are fed. Jesus is quite clear about the significance and centrality of children [Mk 9; 10]. In the Reign of God, children are first. Why is it that almost everywhere in our world, children are last?

Reimagining the Future as the Advent of the Not Yet

Whenever I think of the future, I think of things utopian. As many of you know, the word, utopia, is formed from two Greek words "oú" which means "no" and "tópos" which means place. When we speak of utopia, we speak of something that is possible, but not verifiable. We speak of something that is desired and sought after, but not yet possessed, found or fully realized. A few years ago, a Franciscan sister from Indonesia explained to me that in her language there is no equivalent for the word "no." The closest approximation to the word "no" is found in the phrase "not yet." She related this fact as she told the story of a village woman who, in trying to understand what a Franciscan sister was, asked several questions, beginning with: "Do you have a husband?" and "Do you have children?" Questions to which my friend could only reply, "Not yet!"

This anecdote provides us with a key to understanding "utopia", not as a "no place," but rather, as a "not yet place." Whether speaking of utopia in terms of the ideal school or in terms of the Reign of God, the nature of "not yet-ness" makes it possible for us to hope and to dream for the realization of a human aspiration that is divinely inspired. The primary drawback of utopian thinking is that it does not hold out to us the guarantees of a strategically planned future; rather, it challenges us to live in expectation and readiness for advent, or to be more precise, those advent experiences of our lives, when God breaks into our history, takes us by surprise, and invites us to trust our intuitions that God-with-us is truly God-with-us.

In these seemingly apocalyptic times, when anticipation of the new millennium abounds, we are called by the God of Life to challenge the culture of death. In this Advent of the Not Yet, we are called to confirm through the action of our lives as Catholic educators that our faith will not be undermined by the culture of doubt or co-opted by the culture of absolutism, that our hope will not be eroded by the culture of despair or obscured by a culture of presumption, and that our love will not be threatened by the culture of hate or diminished by the culture of indifference.

Conclusion

In conclusion, I invite you to listen with your heart to these words of wisdom that come to us from the spiritual teachings of Native American elders:

> "*The Wisdomkeepers taught us, the future is here with us today, in the Here and Now. Its coming up in fact, right behind us. Over and over we are told: Turn around and look, there they are, the Seventh Generation --- they're coming up right behind you* (Wall, S. & Arden, H, 1990, p. 120)."

As Catholic educators and administrators, we have been entrusted with a legacy that takes the tears of children seriously. As you ponder your own participation in God's mission, be mindful of those who have tended the bridges before you. Amazed and fearful, may you discover the meaning of fidelity and creativity as you continue to teach as Jesus taught. Indeed, the God of Life is doing something new in this advent of the not yet. In order to perceive it, I urge you to gaze with the eyes of a child. Seven generations from now, may your efforts be remembered.

Excerpts from the Gospel of Mark [RSV]

The people were amazed at the way Jesus taught (1:22).

> *Jesus was not like teachers of the Law, whose ways of knowing were disconnected from reality. Jesus taught with authority, an authority that in our own times might be understood as connected knowing (Belenky, 1986).*

The people were amazed at the way Jesus exorcised (1:27).

> *Jesus gave orders to evil spirits and the spirits obeyed him.*

The people were completely amazed (2:12) at Jesus' authority to forgive sins and to cure the paralyzed.

> *They said "we have never seen anything like this."*

The disciples were terribly afraid (4:41) as they began to wonder who Jesus was and why the wind and the waves obeyed his commands.

> *Jesus asked them directly "Why are you frightened? Are you still without faith? (4:40)"*

The people were all afraid (5:15) when they saw the Gerasene man who used to have a legion of demons within him, sitting before them clothed and in his right mind.

> *They were so frightened they asked Jesus to leave their territory (5:17).*

The people were filled with wonder (amazed) upon hearing the man from Gerasene tell the crowds what Jesus had done for him (5:21).

The woman with the hemorrhage realized that she was cured from her trouble, she came to Jesus, trembling with fear (5:23) and fell at his feet.

> *Though a woman of faith, she experienced fear in the aftermath of being cured.*

In the face of his daughter's death, Jairus was afraid. Jesus, however, exhorts Jairus not to be afraid, but to believe (5:36).

Jairus, his wife, Peter, James, and John (and presumably those excluded from the room) were completely amazed (5:43) when Jesus raised the young girl from the dead.

The people in the synagogue (of Jesus' hometown), upon hearing him preach, were all amazed (6:3).

> *The "extraordinariness" of Jesus' wisdom and ability to work miracles does not correspond to his "ordinariness" of apparent origins. And the people reject him.*

The disciples were afraid when they saw Jesus, whom they believed to be a ghost, walking on the water (6:50).

The disciples were completely amazed and utterly confused (6:51) by the events of the day.

> *Not only had Jesus fed five thousand hungry people, but in the early hours of the morning, knowing of the trouble they were having in their efforts to row against the wind, he walked on water, got into their boat and caused the wind to calm down.*

The people who witnessed Jesus' healing of the man who was deaf and mute, upon hearing the man speak, were completely amazed (7:37).

Peter, James, and John were so frightened (9:6) upon seeing Elijah and Moses talking with Jesus, that Peter did not know what to say.

The disciples, after hearing what was going to happen to Jesus and not understanding what this teaching meant, were afraid to ask him (9:32).

The disciples were completely amazed (10:26) when they heard how hard it is for a rich person to enter the Kingdom of God.

> *This caused them to wonder, "who can be saved?"*

On the road going up to Jerusalem, the disciples were filled with alarm and the people who followed behind were afraid (10:32).

The whole crowd was amazed by Jesus (11:18) teaching after he cleansed the Temple.

The chief priests and teachers of the Law were afraid of Jesus (11:18), precisely because the whole crowd was amazed.

The chief priests, teachers of the Law, and the elders were afraid of the people, because of the people's conviction that John the Baptist was a prophet (11:32).

Thus the authorities were unable to answer the question Jesus posed to them about John's right to baptize.

The Jewish leaders were afraid of the crowd (12:12) and for this reason they decided to leave Jesus alone, rather than having him arrested after he spoke about them through his parable about the vineyard.

The Pharisees and members of Herod's party were (filled with wonder) amazed at Jesus' response (12:17) about rendering to the Emperor what belongs to the Emperor and rendering to God what belongs to God.

Mary Magdalene, Mary the mother of James, and Salome were filled with alarm (16:5) as they entered the open and saw the young man sitting at the right, wearing a robe of white.

They ran from the grave, fearful and amazed. They said nothing to anybody, because they were afraid (16:8).

References

Belenky, M. F. (1986). *Women's Ways of Knowing: The Development of Self, Voice and Mind.* New York: Basic Books.

Oliner, S. & Oliner, P. (1988). *The Altruistic Personality: Rescuers of the Jews in Nazi Europe.* New York: Macmillan.

UNICEF, (1995). *The State of the World's Children.* Oxford: Oxford University Press.

Wall, S. & Arden, H. (1990). *Wisdomkeepers: Meetings with Native American Spiritual Elders.* Hillsboro, Oregon: Beyond Words Publishing.

Chapter 6

Motivating for Change and Renewal

–Robert R. Bimonte, F.S.C.

Do you ever think of yourself as rigid? Inflexible? Unbending? More often than not, we use those words to describe our colleagues or associates. We easily see the problem of "terminal certainty " in others, but seldom in ourselves. The truth, however, is that we are all rigid to one degree or another. None of us wants to give up our secure and familiar ways of being and doing.

One of the things we have learned from current brain research is that the brain is a pattern seeking device. It continually seeks out patterns and stores them. Patterns that are stored and repeated over time become programs. Every pattern you have ever learned since the time you were in your mother's womb is stored in your brain, and the longer those patterns or programs have been with you, the more difficult they are to change. We have patterns as complex as the ways in which we relate to people and as simple as our daily routines and habits; for example, every one of us has a pattern for showering. Each morning, you put the soap in the same hand and wash the same body parts in the same order. That is your showering pattern. If you do not believe this, put the soap in the opposite hand tomorrow morning and see what happens. Most likely, you will lose your balance in the shower. But even more disturbing, when you step out, you will wonder whether or not you are clean. Your patterns are deeply ingrained and they give organization and meaning to our lives. Without them, our world would be confusing and chaotic. They are part of a survival instinct deeply rooted in our reptilian brain whose primary function is to protect us and keep us alive. Is it any wonder that we cling to them so tenaciously?

The Problem Of Rigidity

In many ways, people are defined by their patterns. We are recognized as being generous or selfish, studious or unmotivated by the repeated patterns of behavior and attitude which convey that message. In a similar way, people are defined by what they stand for. In a very real sense, we become rigid whenever we take a passionate stance on an issue or belief and this can be both beneficial and harmful. In a positive light, if you are not rigid, you do not stand for anything. The down side is that if you are too rigid, you might break. When anyone asks us to do or believe something that goes against a strongly held conviction, our normal human response is one of rigidity. Our reptilian brain senses danger and engages our" fight or flight " response. As a result, our blood pressure increases, our heart starts beating faster, and our bodies actually become tense and rigid because our brain perceives such a request as a threat. Sometimes, we mistakenly think that rigidity or clinging to patterns is confined to a particular age group. Depending upon where we find ourselves chronologically, we sometimes tend to characterize the "older" or "younger" generation as being unmovably "set in its ways."

Once again, the truth is that every generation is equally rigid but for different reasons. "Younger" people are rigid because they are inexperienced, idealistic, and scared to death that someone is going to find out that they are not an adult. Remember your own experience as a beginning teacher. Do you remember your first week in the classroom saying to yourself, "I can do this." But all the while, your stomach was churning inside you and you were wondering why you ever got into education in the first place. You felt somewhat like an impostor but you dared not tell anyone because you were afraid of what they would think of you.

Concurrently, many of us adopted rigid behaviors, attitudes, or patterns. We became dogmatic and fashioned ourselves into pseudo-experts who saw only one way of doing things. We were not open to other ways of being or doing. In seeking to bring about change with people in this condition, the best approach is to share with them your own initial struggles and failings. Not only does this humanize you in their eyes, it also opens the door for honest communication. Knowing that you met with real difficulties and survived allows others to drop their own defenses and develop a more open attitude to you and to the program or ideas that you are trying to share.

As we move through the life cycle, "older" people become rigid for different reasons. They become "keepers of the meaning." They see themselves as experienced professionals who have expended a good amount of time and energy creating the person that they have become. Now they want the school, their family, and society in general to sustain and affirm them.

When presenting a new idea or program to these people, you must honor both them and their experience. Never imply that what they do or think is no longer good. If you do that, they hear you telling them that they are no good, and no one wants to hear that. As a result, they become rigid and uninterested in anything you have to say — even if others think it's the greatest idea of the century. The more you can make positive connections to their own experience, the more open they will be to what you have to say.

How Do You Avoid A Rigid Response?

Nine times out of ten, our rigidity is in response to someone asking us to change. Whether you are in your twenties, fifties, or eighties, whenever someone asks you to do something differently, our natural human response is a firm resolve to continue business as usual.

The dilemma is that change is an inevitable part of life as we know it at the end of the twentieth century, and it is only going to become increasingly so as we move into the new millennium. Therefore, we have an obligation to help people to understand that fact and enable them not just to cope, but to grow through creative and constructive change.

In order to understand successful attempts to get people to change, we need only to look at our own experience with personal computers as an example. I would venture to guess that when they were first introduced, almost all of us arched our backs, became quite rigid, and said something like "I can do just fine with my electric typewriter." Writing this essay on my computer, I laugh when I think of myself saying that. The truth is, I would not go back to a typewriter now if my life depended on it! So, how did the computer industry get me to abandon my beloved IBM Selectric? They made their computers "user-friendly." In providing clear step-by-step directions along with a "Help" function, they allowed people to experience success the first time they sat down. By lessening the threat, they lessened the rigidity and opened people up to the possibility of change. Thus, people were ready to now listen to the long-term benefits of using a personal computer. Lessening the fear is the key to getting people to see the long-term benefits of any proposed change.

The implication for staff developers who want to present new ideas is to do everything possible to eliminate threat in order to avoid the normal human response to fear, which is rigidity. Only then, are people ready to hear what you have to say.

Another key element is to honor the person and show respect for his or her knowledge and expertise. Never make someone feel inadequate. If they run into difficulty understanding or performing this new idea or concept, "help" must be readily available, as easily as pressing a button. It cannot be seen as demeaning, but rather as a means to attaining the desired goal. Otherwise, the person will shut down and resist any further attempts at change.

Requirements For Successful Change

Even if you manage to honor the person, lessen their fear, and eliminate threat, the most important thing you have to realize is that no one can make another person change. All we can do is create the right conditions that will predispose people to set a new direction for their lives.

The following four components are absolutely essential to the success of any staff development program:

1. **Desire:** The desire for change is self-generated. Each person has to determine whether or not this new program or behavior is worth the reach. None of us changes because someone else tells us to do so. To some extent we may go through the motions of outward conformity in order to retain our jobs, but deep down nothing changes. There is no real conversion of art or mind. People need to see both the purpose and usefulness of the proposed change. Bear in mind that usefulness is determined by the individual in the here and now. They need to see some immediate benefits for themselves and others before they will even consider the possibility of change. This is why good staff development requires an outstanding initial presentation that will get people excited. Ideally, this should be done by a charismatic presenter who is genuinely excited about the program, can speak with authority, and give real examples of its success based on experience — examples that can be easily replicated and modified.

2. **Vision:** Your audience needs to have a very clear picture of exactly what this new change is. What does it look like? Sound like? Feel like? You must give them a very clear and concrete picture of the proposed change. People cannot hang their hats on abstractions. The vision also needs to be presented enthusiastically. You must be able to demonstrate clearly how this change has improved the quality of education for yourself and your students. The benefits have to be real and tangible, but remember that your presentation must honor and connect to the experience of your audience.

3. **Plan:** Once you have people's interest, you must give them a concise, step-by-step plan to make the vision a

reality. It must be seen as attainable. It is important to consider Madeleine Hunter's theory of the "Hurdles." She very wisely indicates that when you are trying to bring about change, you do not take the teacher who is at the lowest level and place her with the teacher at the highest level. The normal human reaction for anyone in such a situation would be to say that they could not possibly make such a leap. The better way to deal with such a person is to place her with the teacher at the level just above her own. Then the leap seems possible. Any plan that you develop must be perceived as having a logical and sequential step-by-step development. Plans in and of themselves are reassuring, and we must remember that people need to experience success at every step along the way. If too much is expected at first, or if they sense initial failure or undue difficulty, most people will shut down and decide that the change is simply not worth the effort.

4. **Support**: Once people have agreed to implement the desired change, they must be supported along the way. So many plans fail because people met with problems and difficulties along the way and no one was there to offer assistance or answer their questions. That is why single day or one-time in-service programs rarely accomplish anything. It is one thing to get people excited, but we all need support and encouragement in attempting to make the vision a reality. Often, the person who is good at getting people excited during the initial in-service is not the person to do the training or ongoing coaching. The charisma and enthusiasm of that person can sometimes overwhelm people in the initial learning stages. You need people who can gently move people and affirm them every step of the way. Nobody starts as an expert, and each group needs to adapt a proposed change in its own way if they are ever going to develop a sense of ownership. One reason that educational innovations are sometimes short-lived is that after teachers' initial excitement, there was no support system in place to keep them moving forward. If we encounter difficulty and have nowhere to turn, our normal response is to return to the comfort and security of our old patterns.

Then we become even more resistant when someone proposes a new change.

Conclusion

Wonderful and innovative ideas are constantly being generated, but many go nowhere because they are not presented in a way that enables people to respond. The key to successful staff development is to remember that rarely does anyone jump at the idea of change. We must create the proper approach. Then, and only then, can we even hope that our ideas will be received. Change is an inevitable part of life. If you think that things are happening too quickly now, change will occur even more rapidly in the future. Therefore, it is absolutely essential that we understand the nature of patterns and rigidity as well as the most successful approaches to change them. Only those who have the ability to change and adapt will be successful in the twenty-first century.

For further information, you may consult the following sources:

Caine, G.. & Caine, R. (1991). *Making Connections: Teaching and the Human Brain*. Virginia: Association of Supervision and Curriculum Development.

Hart, L. (1983) *Human Brain Development and Human Learning*. Arizona: Books for Educators.

Healy, J. (1990). *Endangered Minds*. New York: Simon and Schuster.

Kovalik, S. (1993). *Integrated Thematic Instruction: The Model*. Arizona: Books for Educators.

The Editors

Rev. Joseph M. O'Keefe, S.J. is an Associate Professor of Education at Boston College, where he coordinates the Catholic School Leadership Program. A former Catholic high school teacher and administrator, he holds a bachelor of arts degree in philosophy from the College of the Holy Cross, a master of arts degree in French literature from Fordham University, as well as a master of divinity degree and a licentiate in sacred theology from Weston Jesuit School of Theology. In 1991 he earned a doctorate from Harvard University in Administration, Planning and Social Policy. He has published on urban education, higher education, school reform, and school leadership. He co-edited *The Contemporary Catholic School: Context, Identity and Diversity* (Falmer, 1996), a comparative study of Catholic schools in the U.S. and England and he is editor of a forthcoming volume of readings on Catholic higher education to be published by Garland Press. With funding from the Lilly Foundation, he is currently completing a nation-wide study of inner-city Catholic schools in the United States. His other on-going research interests include community-service learning, international comparative studies of Catholic schools, and interfaith dialogue. He works closely with educational practitioners as a consultant and school board member. He is also active in parish and campus ministry.

Regina Haney is the Executive Director of the National Association of Boards of Catholic Education (NABE), a commission of the National Catholic Educational Association (NCEA). In this capacity Regina shares her experience with schools and diocesan boards across the country through workshops and publications. In addition, she directs curriculum projects for the association. She coordinated the revision and publication of *AIDS: A Catholic Educational Approach to HIV* and directed the publication of *Faith, Family and Friends, A Catholic Elementary School Guidance Program for Grades K through 8*. She co-edited with Karen Ristau *As We Teach and Learn: Recognizing Our Catholic Identity*, to assist faculty with the integration of Gospel values into the school. During the 1996-1997 school year, she also acted as Director of Chief Administrators of Catholic Education (CACE).

Prior to joining NCEA in 1990, Regina served for nine years as Superintendent of Schools for the Diocese of Raleigh, North Carolina. The strength of her leadership is seen in her many accomplishments as Superintendent. Among them are: the revision and implementation of a system-wide accreditation plan, several publications, including a hands-on science guide for all grade levels; and the establishment of a network of curriculum coordinators. In the area of telecommunications, Regina established a satellite network for all schools in the diocese through which teachers accessed curriculum-based programs, teachers and administrators participated in satellite in-service sessions, many of which were designed and produced by Regina.

For the last six years, she has co-directed New Frontiers, a program to direct school teams to develop a plan to integrate technology into the curriculum.